NEHEMIAH:
GOD'S BUILDER

NEHEMIAH: GOD'S BUILDER

By

RICHARD H. SEUME

MOODY PRESS
CHICAGO

Library of Congress Cataloging in Publication Data

Seume, Richard H.
    Nehemiah: God's builder.

    Bibliography: p. 120.
    1. Nehemiah. 2. Bible. O.T. Nehemiah—Criticism, interpre-
tation, etc. 3. Bible. O.T.—Biography.

BS580.N45S48   221.9'24 [B]   77-29141
ISBN 0-8024-5868-8

The use of selected references from various versions of the
Bible in this publication does not necessarily imply publisher
endorsement of the versions in their entirety.

Contents

Introduction

In retrospect, the book of Nehemiah was a natural for me, for I was the eldest son of an engineer whose designing and drafting skills were devoted to buildings and bridges. If, as Alexander Whyte says of David, "He built the temple every night in his sleep," so it was with my father. Buildings and bridges were his dreams. Steel and rivets were the skeletal stuff which made those dreams come true.

It was only natural then that some of that dream stuff would filter into the stream of the family, until my father's life was cut short in the midst of years. But he lived long enough before the Lord took him to give me both the desire and the design to be a kind of builder myself. During my ministry, when the blessing of God required that we build, I was thrilled with the prospect of having a part in the erection of a fitting temple for my God and His people.

On such occasions I naturally turned to the book of Nehemiah for both inspiration and instruction. He had been a builder long before me. There, in the book which bears his name, I found Nehemiah's personal diary. As Bernhard W. Anderson reminds us in his *Understanding the Old Testament*, "This is the only example of the continuous story of a man's career, written in the style of an autobiography, that we have in the Old Testament. It is a historical record of the greatest importance; and as a narrative, it is . . . fresh and interesting."[1]

I have accordingly placed Nehemiah's record in italics so as to present the appearance of a handwritten record.

7

It has been wisely observed that before our message is of any use there must be a sense of need. Once that need has been established, the corollary is clear: Drive home the message until there is no possible refuge from its application!

It seems appropriate, therefore, at the outset of this series of memoirs from Nehemiah, to ask: Where is there a *need* for this book? What possible applications can we draw from his message now that we are twenty-five centuries removed from the events recorded there?

These are legitimate questions and deserve appropriate answers. Let me state what I believe should always be the answer to such questions. To believe in the divine inspiration of Holy Scripture is to put ourselves to school with every part of the Bible—the Old Testament as well as the New. This book of Nehemiah is a part of that sacred library given by inspiration of God the Holy Spirit. Because Nehemiah is inspired, his book is therefore "useful for teaching the faith and correcting error, for resetting the direction of a man's life and training him in good living. The Scriptures are the comprehensive equipment of the man of God, and fit him fully for all branches of his work" (2 Tim 3:16-17, Phillips). Therefore if we were to omit this book from our study of the Bible, we would lose something which has been designed by the Spirit of God for our development in Christian maturity and ministry.

Having said this, however, I am aware that some portions of the Bible hold a greater attraction for the believer than others. For that reason, Nehemiah may not at this time be one of your favorites. You are not alone in feeling this way. Alexander Whyte, whose *Bible Characters* remains one of the classic collections on the subject, makes this admission about Nehemiah:

> For a long time I was not much drawn to Nehemiah. I did not aright understand Nehemiah, and I did not love him. He was not my kind, as we say: the kind, that is, that I like best to read about, and to think about, and to imitate and to preach. I thought of him, if a patriotic, at the same time, an outside, a

surface, a hard, and an austere man. And, worst of all, a man who was always pleased with himself; the first of Pharisees. . . . I should have remembered what Canon Gore puts so well in *Lux Mundi,* "At starting, each of us, according to our disposition, is conscious of liking some books of Scripture better than others. This, however, should lead us to recognize that, in some way we specially need the teaching that is less attractive to us. We should set ourselves to study what we less like, till that, too, has had its proper effect in moulding our conscience and shaping our character."[2]

With these preliminary observations as background, it is my hope that whatever may be our initial attitude toward Nehemiah, we may come to see the need for including this book in our private and public study. I also hope we may come to love the man and his ministry as set forth in his memoirs.

1

The Architect's Plan

Nehemiah is a builder's book. Let us therefore begin with the architect's plan, the examination of which should give us essential background for what will follow.

In the first place, it would be well to consider a basic aspect of the book, that is, its *historical plane*.

Once in the history of mankind, a man told a nation its history in detail, predicting the near and distant future so distinctly that both seemed to lie equally close to his eye on the map of events. That man was Moses. That nation was Israel. And that prediction has been preserved for us in Deuteronomy, chapters 28-30.

In essence, Moses foretold four things which were unprecedented, inconsistent with each other, and to human reason absurd. He predicted that Israel would drive out all the nations which inhabited the land of Canaan. While there, if they obeyed Jehovah's laws, they would enjoy the blessing of God and the fruit of the land. If, however, they were disobedient to His commandments, they and their land would wither under every curse that could strike man, and they would be driven out. But should they repent and return to Jehovah, He would have mercy on them and restore them to their land.

Every jot and tittle of those predictions came to pass. Israel did possess Canaan (Josh 1—12), but subsequent disobedience led to defeat and eventual deliverance into Babylonian captivity. Later, when their hearts were changed, God moved a pagan monarch to issue a remarkable decree permitting their return to their homeland. That royal edict read as follows: "Thus saith Cyrus king of Persia, All the kingdoms of the earth hath the LORD God of heaven given me; and he hath charged me to build him an house in Jerusalem, which is in Judah. Who is there among you of all his people? The LORD his God be with him, and let him go up" (2 Chron 36:23; Ezra 1:1-3).

The rest is history.

To review the story of the return as briefly as possible, let us concentrate on three figures and three events. First, in 540 B.C., some fifty thousand Jews rallied to the initial call of Zerubbabel, a prince of Judah in captivity, and returned with him to rebuild the *Temple*. Some eighty years later, a second contingent went back with Ezra, a priest, to restore the *worship* of Jehovah. Finally, in about 445 B.C., the last phalanx joined a man named Nehemiah, and together they returned to restore the *walls and gates* of the beloved city of God.

From this brief scenario of Israel's history, we may learn an important truth. God is a gentleman; He always keeps His word. Everything He said to His people regarding blessing in the land, dispersion because of disobedience, and subsequent restoration when there was repentance, came to pass precisely as He promised.

As we read Nehemiah and its companion books, Ezra and Esther, we receive the final message of the Old Testament in *history,* and in their counterparts, Haggai, Zechariah, and Malachi, the final word of the Old Testament in *prophecy.* These six books stand at the chronological close of the Old Testament.

The same God who preserved the book of Nehemiah as a standing witness to the immutability of His Word to His ancient people Israel, has also revealed in writing His plan for this world—a plan He intends to consummate according to His divine purpose.

Second, let us say a word about the *personal plane* of the

book. Here we are thinking specifically about the man Nehemiah. Of his personal history we know little beyond what he has told us in the book. He was the son of Hachaliah, which distinguishes him from others who bore the same name (Ezra 2:2; Neh 3:16). He was one of the children of the captivity, born and brought up in the furnace of affliction. Through circumstances not revealed, Nehemiah rose to a position of eminence in the Persian court as the king's cupbearer. Thus this remarkable man came into a position of influence where his latent gifts could be developed and honed for later use.

As the story unfolds, it becomes evident that Nehemiah was a man of profound piety. He related everything whether large or small to the desire to do the will of God, in whose presence he lived and moved. This is attested more than once by the interjectional prayers which appear throughout the book.

Nehemiah's unselfish spirit is equally significant. Whatever wealth he possessed he used for public ends, and there is not the slightest reference to self apart from the common good. His public administration evidenced the energy, sagacity, and even severity which guided the demands of his vocation. No wonder that ancient Jewish tradition gives Nehemiah a place of honor no less than that accorded Ezra.

We see that the man Nehemiah is inseparably welded to his ministry. We must not fail to see also that God works His plan by working His people. That principle remains today. The moment is always ripe for some new Nehemiah—or whoever—to hear that word which was spoken out of the living experience of a man of God, "The world has yet to see what God can do with and through and in a man who is fully consecrated to Him!" To which that man, be he Dwight Lyman Moody, or anyone, may reply, "By the grace of God, I'll be that man!"

In the third place, let us view from the *spiritual plane* the need for Nehemiah's memoirs. Here we must ask the question: What *problem* confronted God's servant when he left the splendor and comfort of the Persian court to return to the city of his fathers? Furthermore, what did he purpose to do about it? Little is gained by being exposed to a problem if one is not prepared to seek a solution. It was within that framework that Nehemiah faced his task.

The problem was twofold: ruin and reproach. The walls of Jerusalem lay in shambles. Without a true national and spiritual center of reference, the people were in disarray. When Nehemiah, in his far-off exile, heard of conditions in the holy city, his heart was moved. In due course his whole life and abilities were concentrated on the work of reconstructing both city and people. Reconstruction is the key word of the book. My honored friend, J. Sidlow Baxter, calls the book of Nehemiah "The Book of Reconstruction." It is a builder's book.

The problem which faced our friend Nehemiah is essentially with us even now. Realism compels us to recognize that individually, nationally, and internationally, ruin and reproach characterize the world's condition. All news media available remind us that our depravity is showing. Broken walls there are. And burned gates. Even the church of God has her special problems and needs help. So do we as individual believers. I like to think of Jerusalem as symbolic of that sacred city in the heart of every true child of God. As we face up to our condition, conscience brings home disturbing tidings about ourselves. If we are honest, we must admit that, here and there, all is not well. A gate is burned here; the wall is broken there. We reflect on what we might be, or ought to be, and sigh with Tennyson,

> Ah, for a man to arise in me,
> That the man I am might cease to be!
> ALFRED LORD TENNYSON

Mind you, there is nothing unusual or strange about this awakening of the soul. Indeed, it is a noble exercise, born out of the conviction that things ought to be different and better, and the desire by the help of God to make them so. That is the work of reconstruction in us. I believe that a careful reading of the book of Nehemiah will give us not only the inspiration for a constructive useful life in our generation, but the instructions we need to bring it to pass.

Consonant with the things we have said thus far to support the need for this study, it is imperative that we include some word about the *prophetic plane*. For obvious reasons, we will confine our attention to Israel and her future. At once we are confronted with a question which does not admit of easy answers. There are those who deny that Israel exists today; these claim therefore that she has no future as a nation. Others will acknowledge Israel as a race, but not as a nation. Still others, by and large numbered among premillenarians, believe that Israel not only remains as a race, but also has a glorious future as a nation in a coming Kingdom age.

Our study in Nehemiah suddenly leaps into relevance. We observed the unfolding of history in the return of that remnant under Zerubbabel, Ezra, and Nehemiah. We also see the prophetic forecast confirming that a day is coming when God will again bring Israel out of her "graves" (those nations where she is now in exile) and restore her to her own land.

For us living in this generation, such a prospect seems reasonable. Since May 14, 1948, Israel has been an independent state within the limits of the United Nations. This is remarkable. For the first time since A.D. 70, Israel is recognized as a political state. Dr. John F. Walvoord has written,

> The restoration of Israel to its ancient land and its establishment as a political government is almost without parallel in the history of the world. Never before has an ancient people, scattered for so many centuries, been able to return to their ancient land and re-establish themselves with such success and swift progress as is witnessed in the new state of Israel.[1]

Obviously this is only the beginning of the consummation of the divine program for Israel. A visit to the valley of dry bones

set forth in Ezekiel 37:1-14 makes this clear. The prophet
Obadiah adds his own inspired word when he promises that in
that future day, "The house of Jacob shall possess their pos-
sessions" (Obad 17).

According to the prophetic forecast, three events of major
significance will occur. First, regathered Israel will be restored
to her land—a land *promised* to Abraham (Gen 12:1,) *provided* through the military conquests of Joshua (Josh 1—14),
and *preserved* unto the present hour despite numerous attempts
by contiguous hostile nations to extirpate Israel from the earth.

Second, Israel, having returned in unbelief will be reconciled
to Jehovah. According to Zechariah, "In that day there shall
be a fountain opened to the house of David and to the inhabitants of Jerusalem for sin and for uncleanness" (Zech 13:1),
and a nation will be born again in a day.

Finally—at long last—Israel will fulfill her original purpose
as the world's blesser. Until now, her presence in the earth has
been a malediction, but in that day she will be a benediction, for
through her "shall all families of the earth be blessed" (Gen
12:3). Additional passages such as Zechariah 8:13, 20-23 and
Zephaniah 3:19-20 assure us of this.

Mary Ann Thompson seemed to sigh for that day when she
wrote,

> O Zion, haste,
> thy mission high fulfilling.

In the light of history and prophecy, we need have no fear.
Israel will!

We have considered the architect's plan. We have viewed
in succession the historical, the personal, the spiritual, and the
prophetic planes of this plan. In conclusion, let us reflect upon
the *practical plane.* Here I should like to share a contemporary
illustration.

In the book *Daktar/Diplomat in Bangladesh,* Dr. Viggo
Olsen relates his experience when constructing some four thou-

sand houses as a medical facility for serving physical and spiritual needs in that land. In the prospect of such a venture, Dr. Olsen began to read the book of Nehemiah. He writes,

> I spent every spare moment, thinking through how to organize the brigade's work in such a way that we actually could complete the four thousand houses. . . . Early on the morning of April 15, as I read the tedious third chapter of Nehemiah, two principles suddenly leaped out of those pages at me—principles which showed me how the work of the Bangladesh Brigade should be organized. . . . The chapter, ordinarily considered one of the least interesting chapters in the Bible, merely listed the groups of people working together, side by side, rebuilding the wall of the holy city of Jerusalem. I was struck, however, that no expert builders were listed. . . . If those amateurs could complete the wall of Jerusalem in fifty-two days, then we also, despite our lack of expertise, should be able to complete our work in fifty-two days. . . . The Nehemiah passage also imparted another principle: instead of each team doing the same small phase of the work, assembly-line style, in village after village, each team must, instead, manage and supervise the total operation in its target villages from initial survey to final inspection of completed houses. . . . With these principles as our guidelines . . . we put together our house-building system.[2]

Thus through this dedicated doctor and his colleagues the Bangladesh Brigade became a reality, and is now serving the people of that land.

Here is a true successor to Nehemiah. And it was Nehemiah's book that helped him.

To conclude, we agree with John C. Whitcomb, Jr.:

> No portion of the Old Testament provides us with a greater incentive to dedicated, discerning zeal for the work of God than the Book of Nehemiah. The example of Nehemiah's passion for the truth of God's Word, whatever the cost or consequences, is an example sorely needed in the present hour.[3]

That is a true word. May it please God to raise up others who will follow in Nehemiah's train. Our times desperately need them.

2

Sharpening the Axe

In his devotional volume, *Filled With the Spirit,* Richard Ellsworth Day makes this perceptive observation:

> It would be no surprise, if a study of secret causes were undertaken, to find that every golden era in human history proceeds from the devotion and righteous passion of some single individual. This does not set aside the sovereignty of God; it simply indicates the instrument through which He uniformly works. There are no bona fide mass movements; it just looks that way. At the center of the column there is always one man who knows His God, and knows where he is going.[1]

This is not difficult to divine. *Men* are God's method. While the church may be looking for better *methods,* God is looking for better men. Consider these fragments from the prophets: "Run ye to and fro through the streets of Jerusalem, and see now, and know, and seek in the broad places thereof, if ye can find a man, if there be any that executeth judgment, that seeketh the truth" (Jer 5:1). "And I sought for man among them, that should make up the hedge, and stand in the gap before me for the land, that I should not destroy it: but I found none" (Ezek 22:30).

Fortunately, in the case before us now, God found a man. His name was Nehemiah. But the axe had to be sharpened before it could do its work.

When God wants to drill a man,
And thrill a man,
And skill a man,
When God wants to mold a man
To play the noblest part;
When He yearns with all His heart
To create so great and bold a man
That all the world shall be amazed,
Watch His methods, watch His ways!
How He ruthlessly perfects
Whom He royally elects!
How He hammers him and hurts him,
And with mighty blows converts him
Into trial shapes of clay which
Only God understands;
While his tortured heart is crying
And he lifts beseeching hands!
How He bends but never breaks
When his good He undertakes;
How He uses whom He chooses,
And with every purpose fuses him;
By every act induces him
To try His splendor out—
God knows what He's about.

AUTHOR UNKNOWN

As we might suspect, the initial memoir gives a vivid account of that sharpening process. Three areas are to be considered.

In the first place, observe Nehemiah's *position*. He describes it very simply and without fanfare at the end of his first memoir: *"For I was the king's cupbearer."*

A cupbearer was not a new court functionary. Pharaoh, king of Egypt in the days of Joseph, had one. He is mentioned in Genesis 40:21. Nehemiah was cupbearer to the king of Persia, Artaxerxes Longimanus, the son of Ahasuerus (Xerxes) who took Esther to be queen in the place of Vashti. The position held by Nehemiah was not one of political rank. He was not a minister of state like Joseph or Daniel, but as a court servant he did hold a place of special privilege and responsibility.[2] The cupbearer, in at least one way, was the protector of his sovereign. He was required to taste the royal wine before it was given to the king lest the monarch should be poisoned by some treacherous enemy. In this way, cupbearers became royal favorites.

Just how Nehemiah came into this position of favor is not clear; his memoir does not tell us. We can only conjecture that, "like Daniel and his trio of compatriots, and like Ezra, his own colleague, Nehemiah was a child of the Captivity. . . . They were all children in whom was no blemish, but wellfavored, and skilful in all wisdom and knowledge . . . and such as had ability to stand in the king's palace."[3] Whatever the reason, there he was. In his own way, Nehemiah was living witness to the promise of the proverb, "A man's gift maketh room for him, and bringeth him before great men" (Prov 18:16). Nehemiah's fidelity to his position of trust before the king guaranteed similar fidelity in a more responsible and difficult task yet to come.

Here is a challenge to all of us who know the saving grace of God provided through our Lord Jesus Christ. With that grace has come the gift of the Holy Spirit to us, not only to indwell but also to enable us to serve our generation by the will of God before high and low alike.

We come now to the second important matter in this memoir: Nehemiah's *posture* (Neh 1:1-4).

> *The words of Nehemiah the son of Hachaliah. And it came to pass in the month Chisleu, in the twentieth year, as I was in Shushan the palace, that Hanani, one of my brethren, came, he and certain men of Judah; and I asked them concerning the Jews that had escaped, which were left of the captivity, and concerning Jerusalem. And they said unto me, The remnant that are left of the captivity there in the province are in great affliction and reproach: the wall of Jerusalem also is broken*

*down, and the gates thereof are burned with fire. And it came
to pass, when I heard these words, that I sat down and wept,
and mourned certain days, and fasted, and prayed before the
God of heaven,*

"Nehemiah plunges into his story, without giving us any hints
of his previous history."[4] "He was in the palace, or better, the
fortress at Susa, the winter retreat of the Persian monarchs.
Susa was an Elamite city, eighty miles east of the Tigris River,
and within sight of the Bakhtiyari Mountains. Here was the
great audience hall similar to another hall at Persepolis.[5]

In November or December—Chislev in the text—while Nehemiah was serving in the royal court, one of his brethren,
Hanani, with a group of his companions of Judah, came to him.
The language here used will allow us to regard Hanani as only
a more or less distant relative of Nehemiah, but later reference
to him at Jerusalem as "my brother Hanani" (7:2) suggests
that his own brother was meant.[6]

The decision of these men to seek out Nehemiah is a matter
of considerable interest. Why Nehemiah? After all, there was
a substantial Jewish community at Susa. Nevertheless, Hanani
and his friends sought out Nehemiah, one who evidently en-
joyed a good reputation among his own people and was a man
of influence at court as well.

To Nehemiah they brought the grim news concerning Jerusalem and its remnant inhabitants. The people were in reproach
and great affliction. Dispirited and defeated, they lacked desire
to restore the city. And not only this. The city walls lay in
ruins, and the gates were burned—an awful reminder to Nehemiah of the danger which threatened his beloved people at the
hands of hostile and vicious neighbors. It was a sad report
indeed.[7]

How did Nehemiah receive it? He might have dismissed
these men and their distressing tidings with the response, "It's
too bad. What a tragic ending to the once glorious city of David

and Solomon. But I must not mourn; Persia is now my country. Here are my career and my destiny." But Nehemiah did not do that. He specifically "asked" his companions about the state of Jerusalem (1:2) suggesting that amid the delicacies of his court life, his thoughts often returned to the ancient home of his people.

How are we to explain this part of the man? Obviously, he possessed a strong sense of *nationalism*. The Jews and Jerusalem were written indelibly on his heart. With the psalmist he could say, "If I forget thee, O Jerusalem, let my right hand forget her cunning. If I do not remember thee, let my tongue cleave to the roof of my mouth; if I prefer not Jerusalem above my chief joy" (Psalm 137:5-6).

And for good reason. Adeney writes, "The great anxiety of the Jews about the bodies of their dead, and their horror of the exposure of a corpse, made them look with peculiar concern on the tombs of their people."[8] In this present circumstance, then, Nehemiah was simply sharing the sentiment of his people. He longed to guard and honor the last resting-places of his kin. Any danger to the sepulchers of his fathers could only be met with the greatest distress. It is clear from the story that this was precisely Nehemiah's response. Night and day he sat and wept, mourned and fasted, thus to share the sorrows of his countrymen.

Beyond his nationalism, one more thing must be said about this man. Nehemiah also had a deep *spiritual involvement*. His name suggests this: "consolation of Jehovah." He was plainly a man with a burden. Prophets such as Habakkuk shared this experience. Habakkuk's little prophecy opens with these ominous words, "The burden which Habakkuk the prophet did see" (Hab 1:1). The prophet Malachi wrote "The burden of the word of the LORD to Israel by Malachi" (Mal 1:1).

I believe it can be said that the *burden* constitutes a man's warrant for preaching or serving the Lord in any capacity. The biographer of the late Phillips Brooks notes that, immediately before going into the pulpit, "he appeared like one burdened with a message from God" when he was in travail to discharge

Where there is no burden, one cannot but wonder, can there be blessing?

Nehemiah had a burden. In the words of the poet, he could honestly say, "With my burden, I begin."

This brings us to the final movement in the first memoir, Nehemiah's *pursuit*. It was prayer. Had his response to the melancholy news been only grief, we should witness merely a demonstration of patriotic sentiment. Such would be expected of any loyal Jew. But Nehemiah at prayer lifted the whole matter into much higher meaning and interest. Out of deference to the man and his intercessory outpouring, let us pause and listen (1:5-11).

> *And said, I beseech thee, O Lord God of heaven, the great and terrible God, that keepeth covenant and mercy for them that love him and observe his commandments: let thine ear now be attentive, and thine eyes open, that thou mayest hear the prayer of thy servant, which I pray before thee now, day and night, for the children of Israel thy servants, and confess the sins of the children of Israel, which we have sinned against thee: both I and my father's house have sinned. We have dealt very corruptly against thee, and have not kept the commandments, nor the statutes, nor the judgments, which thou commandedst thy servant Moses. Remember, I beseech thee, the word that thou commandedst thy servant Moses, saying, If ye transgress, I will scatter you abroad among the nations: But if ye turn unto me, and keep my commandments, and do them; though there were of you cast out unto the uttermost part of the heaven, yet will I gather them from thence, and will bring them unto the place that I have chosen to set my name there. Now these are thy servants and thy people, whom thou hast redeemed by thy great power, and by thy strong hand. O Lord, I beseech thee, let now thine ear be attentive to the prayer of thy servant, and to the prayer of thy servants, who desire to*

> *fear thy name: and prosper, I pray thee, thy servant this day,
> and grant him mercy in the sight of this man.*

Two things stand out in that prayer. In the first place, it provides insight into the reason for Israel's calamities and into the relation of Jehovah to these calamities. Also its form, as Adeney observes, is a combination of three elements: "the language of devotion cultivated by Persian sages; expressions culled from the venerated Hebrew law-book, Deuteronomy; and new phrases called out by the new needs of the immediate occasion."[9]

The body of the prayer reveals at once something of the orderliness of this layman's thoughts. He began with a remarkable expression of adoration of God, and Adeney suggests the wording seems more Persian than Jewish. *"I beseech thee, O Lord God of heaven, the great and terrible God."* Those words *"God of heaven"* were favorites with Nehemiah.[10] When he described his interview with the king, he said, *" So I prayed to the God of heaven"* (2:4). Adeney also points out that later on, when in conflict with his enemies, he answered their mockery by avowing, *"The God of heaven, he will prosper us"* (2:20).

Most important, Nehemiah affirmed at the outset the majesty of God. This was something devout Jews treasured; they never permitted their devotions to slip into familiarity. The revelation of the fatherhood of God which is given to us in Jesus Christ in no way diminishes the need for awe in our address to Him. Our Father He is indeed, but the model prayer continues with "which art in heaven, hallowed be thy name" (Matt 6:9). Nehemiah moved from worship to the need of the hour. Probably memory of the book of Deuteronomy provoked him to plead both God's covenant promises to His people and His mercy. He perceived that the two go together. Nehemiah believed that God is to be trusted; there is no credibility gap with Him.

Having laid bare his heart before such a One, Nehemiah

plunged at once into confession of sin. He did not complain about the cruel behavior of the enemies of his people; the real enemy was to be found within their own ranks.[11] Note that Nehemiah prayed, *"We have sinned against thee: both I and my father's house have sinned"* (1:6). His confession was both corporate and personal. Like Daniel and Ezra, Nehemiah dared to identify himself with his people though he was far from them.

Observe two points in his confession. First, he acknowledged that their sin had been against God. This is as it should be. David teaches us this in his familiar plea for pardon: "Against thee, thee only, have I sinned, and done this evil in thy sight" (Psalm 51:4). Maclaren asks, "How could David have thought of his sin, which had in so many ways been 'against' others, as having been 'against Thee, Thee only'?" He answers, "David's deed had been a crime against Bathsheba, against Uriah, against his family and realm; but these were not its blackest characteristics. Every crime against man is sin against God."[12] The New Testament prodigal adds his own confession: "Father, I have sinned against heaven, and in thy sight" (Luke 15:21).

In the second place, Nehemiah's confession took a positive position, and he reflected upon the promises of God. Here he drew heavily upon the words of Moses, which would be perfectly natural in time of national penitence and hope for restoration. I like his expression at the beginning of verse 8: *"Remember, I beseech thee, the word."* To be sure, it was a "word" of *retribution* for disobedience, and Nehemiah did not close his eyes to the fact. God had said in another place that the way of the transgressor is hard, and Israel was paying a heavy price for her transgressions. But it was also a "word" of *redemption*. This dear man reminded the Lord that His people are those whom He *has redeemed by his great power and strong hand* (1:10). When sin has been confessed and forsaken, it is divine grace that opens the heart of God and provides a way home.

Nehemiah reminded God of this word as well, and dared to importune for his people using God's own words, "If ye turn unto me . . . yet will I gather them . . . and will bring them unto the place that I have chosen to set my name there" (1:9). His prayer for his beloved people was rooted in the promises of God. Adeney points out that having embraced the wider circle of the nation, Nehemiah, only at the very last, in little more than a sentence, mentioned his own personal petition.[13] *"O Lord, I beseech thee, let now thine ear be attentive to the prayer of thy servant, and to the prayer of thy servants, who desire to fear thy name: and prosper, I pray thee, thy servant this day, and grant him mercy in the sight of this man."*

Nehemiah was really saying that the outpourings of his heart were prompted by a decision, an act of personal dedication, for whatever the Lord might require of His servant. Nehemiah must himself seek release to go and help his dispirited people and the devastated city.

In a very simple but solemn manner, God had been quietly at work, chiseling and grinding to hone a man to do a job. The axe was now sharpened; the instrument is ready for the task. Nehemiah was prepared at last to "play the noblest part."

3

Surveying the Situation

Now it was April, Nisan according to the Jewish calendar. Some four months had elapsed since Hanani's unexpected visit with his unwelcome news about the situation in the homeland. That visit had brought Nehemiah to his knees in confession and earnest supplication to the God of heaven. But now the time had come to act. This new memoir depicts God's servant on his feet ready to be involved in the forthcoming drama of deliverance of his people. The moment for which he had been prepared of God was at hand.

With a brief word of introduction, Nehemiah plunges into his memoir (2:1-4).

> And it came to pass in the month Nisan, in the twentieth year of Artaxerxes the king, that wine was before him: and I took up the wine, and gave it unto the king. Now I had not been beforetime sad in his presence. Wherefore the king said unto me, Why is thy countenance sad, seeing thou art not sick? this is nothing else but sorrow of heart. Then I was very sore afraid, and said unto the king, Let the king live for ever: why should not my countenance be sad, when the city, the place of my fathers' sepulchres, lieth waste, and the gates thereof are consumed with fire? Then the king said unto me, For what dost thou make request? So I prayed to the God of heaven.

That Persian king was perceptive. Mark again the two questions he raised: "Why is thy countenance sad, seeing thou art not sick? . . . For what dost thou make request?" They bear close scrutiny.

A cupbearer's office required washing the royal goblet, tasting the royal wine, and then handing it to the king. To do this, obviously, meant appearing before his sovereign in person. Court etiquette forbade him doing so with a sad face; cupbearers were expected to be stouthearted men in stout bodies. Shakespeare puts this thought on the lips of Julius Caesar when he says,

> Let me have men about me that are fat,
> Sleek-headed men, and such as sleep o'nights;
> Yon Cassius hath a lean and hungry look;
> He thinks too much: such men are dangerous.[1]

Nehemiah was plainly a sad man. His face bore visual evidence of deep grief. The king sensed this, and raised the questions. The closing words of verse 2 indicate that Nehemiah was frightened: *"Then I was very sore afraid."* Well he might have been. His petition would be uncommon, especially after the decree of Ezra 4:21. There we read that the king had issued the following royal order: "Give ye now commandment to cause these men [that is, the Jews] to cease, and that this city be not builded, until another commandment shall be given from me." Inasmuch as that order had not been rescinded, to request permission to leave the royal court might be construed as impertinence. Worse still, the king might interpret this display of gloom as a sinister exposure of possible treason. Understandably Nehemiah was afraid as he handed the royal goblet to the king.

To his delight, however, God gave His servant favor with the monarch. Instead of driving Nehemiah from his table, he made surprising inquiry: *"For what dost thou make request?"* Here was a second occasion for anxiety. In that brief moment before answering, Nehemiah shot one of many arrows of prayer to heaven. He realized that his hopes for his people hung on that question and, more particularly, on the king's reply.

This brings us to the first major section of the second memoir which I have chosen to call *the request* (2:5-6, 8).

> *And I said unto the king, If it please the king, and if thy servant have found favour in thy sight, that thou wouldest send me unto Judah, unto the city of my fathers' sepulchres, that I may build it. And the king said unto me, (the queen also sitting by him,) For how long shall thy journey be? and when wilt thou return? So it pleased the king to send me; and I set him a time. . . . And the king granted me, according to the good hand of my God upon me.*

How could Artaxerxes now sanction the building of the wall of Jerusalem when a few years earlier he had expressly forbidden its construction (Ezra 4:21)? Perhaps the answer lies in the fact that the king's present action, following Nehemiah's request, did not withdraw the former decree that construction of the wall be stopped. That order had been executed. The decree also had made provision for possible subsequent permission to resume building: "until another commandment shall be given from me." Now that the king had satisfied himself that a trusted servant would superintend the operation, he felt free to issue a new order.[2]

The king was so thoroughly convinced of Nehemiah's integrity that he granted him everything he requested, including royal authorization, a set time for the project, materials with which to build, safe conduct visas through unfriendly territory, and a personal letter of introduction to the governors west of the Euphrates river.

Nehemiah's last word concerning his generous interview with Artaxerxes concludes with a phrase typical of this godly man, *"And the king granted me, according to the good hand of my God upon me"* (2:8). This man did not put his confidence in princes; his trust was in the Lord. God heard his prayer, the request was granted, and Nehemiah was on his way—*sent, safe,* and *supplied.*

Before leaving this point, notice the language of Nehemiah's request; it deserves emphasis. *"Send me to Judah,"* he pleads, *"that I may build it."* Here is the answer to the problem referred to in the initial memoir. Here, too, is a vital principle of Scripture. To the church at Rome Paul wrote, "Let us therefore follow after the things which make for peace, and things wherewith one may edify another," (Rom 14:19). Again, this time to the Corinthian believers, he said, "Let all things be done unto edifying," (1 Cor 14:26).

What do these texts teach? The importance of building up, which is what edification means. The Greek root form of "edify" means, literally, *to make a house.* Wycliffe used the term in his rendering of Genesis 2:22, "The LORD God edified the rib which he took of Adam, into a woman." Paul typically used the word to mean building up spiritually.

Nehemiah wanted to edify. He was a builder.

At verse 10 we come to the second part of this excerpt, *the resistance.* There we pick up Nehemiah's memoir:

> *When Sanballat the Horonite, and Tobiah the servant, the Ammonite, heard of it, it grieved them exceedingly that there was come a man to seek the welfare of the children of Israel.*

It is always so. Whenever someone appears on the horizon and announces, "Let us rise and build," someone else always answers, "Let us rise and break!" There is no opportunity without opposition. For every job done by the servant of God, there is a job by the enemy of the gospel.

No one knew this better than Paul. Writing to the Corinthian church, he said, "I shall stay here in Ephesus until the feast of Pentecost, for there is a great opportunity of doing useful work, and there are many people against me" (1 Cor 16:9, Phillips).

What was the grievance of these critics against Nehemiah?

His coming did not directly involve them. But they hated the Jews, and the prospect of favor being shown the Jews grieved them. In addition, they feared that Jerusalem might regain eminence in Palestine.

In the days of the young church, the religious leaders reacted in the same way. As Peter and John spoke to the people explaining the cure of the lame man, the priests and the captain of the temple, together with the Sadducees, came upon them, "being grieved that they taught the people, and preached through Jesus the resurrection from the dead" (Acts 4:1-2).

That has a familiar sound. Anyone who has been involved in a spiritual building program for the Kingdom of God knows that critics, like the poor, are ever with us.

But let them grieve. Nehemiah must go. And go he did. His memoir continues, *"So I came to Jerusalem, and was there three days"* (2:11).

This brings us to a third matter, the *review* (2:12-16).

> *And I arose in the night, I and some few men with me; neither told I any man what my God had put in my heart to do at Jerusalem: neither was there any beast with me, save the beast that I rode upon. And I went out by night by the gate of the valley, even before the dragon well, and to the dung port, and viewed the walls of Jerusalem, which were broken down, and the gates thereof were consumed with fire. Then I went on to the gate of the fountain, and to the king's pool: but there was no place for the beast that was under me to pass. Then went I up in the night by the brook, and viewed the wall, and turned back, and entered by the gate of the valley, and so returned. And the rulers knew not whither I went, or what I did; neither had I as yet told it to the Jews, nor to the priests, nor to the nobles, nor to the rulers, nor to the rest that did the work.*

Armed with royal authority, thrilled with a sense of Jehovah's overruling all obstacles, and recognizing the immensity of the task before him, Nehemiah set out on his survey. Because of the threat of the enemy, he did not broadcast his intentions save to a handful of trusted men. Furthermore, he made his survey under cover of darkness. In these ways, he was free to determine the real condition of things. Until now his information had been only hearsay.

The route Nehemiah followed and the records he made confirmed all he had heard from his brother, Hanani. The sight which met his gaze was dismal. The great wall was indeed broken down; the gates were consumed with fire. Step by step, the builder and his little band made their circuit of the city. Then they returned to the valley gate from whence they had set out. The verdict was in; the worst had been confirmed. Tomorrow Nehemiah would share his burden with his people.

Two things were gained by such a survey. In the first place, Nehemiah gathered information that he would need for the task ahead. "Nothing is more terrible," observes Goethe, "than *active ignorance.*" A practical man, Nehemiah must know for himself, and he must know the worst.[3] That night ride confirmed his fears that his beloved city needed help.

In addition, Nehemiah's action draws attention to the importance of the unhurried view. Our Lord taught us to consider a thing carefully, lest our faith be presumptuous. "For which of you, intending to build a tower, sitteth not down first, and counteth the cost, whether he have sufficient to finish it? Lest haply, after he hath laid the foundation, and is not able to finish it, all that behold it begin to mock him, Saying, This man began to build, and was not able to finish" (Luke 14:28-30).

Nehemiah felt that way. He would not begin to build until he was certain of the cost. Once that was ascertained, he would not stop until he had finished his work. He was a wise master builder, and the engineer in him was emerging.

Having presented his request, having faced initial resistance—Have no fear; there is more to come!—and having made his adventurous night ride, Nehemiah was now ready to sound *reveille.* Again we shall consult the memoir (2:17-18).

*Then said I unto them, Ye see the distress that we are in,
how Jerusalem lieth waste, and the gates thereof are burned
with fire: come, and let us build up the wall of Jerusalem, that
we be no more a reproach. Then I told them of the hand of
my God which was good upon me; as also the king's words that
he had spoken unto me.*

What a remarkable call to arms that was. Observe that, first,
Nehemiah *identified* himself with the need. *"Ye see the distress
that we are in."* If the task were ever to be undertaken, the
reformer must infuse a "Divine discontent." Furthermore, he
must be willing to include himself in the project. Observe that
he did not use the first person singular, for he could not do the
work alone. Nor did he employ the second person: "You must
do it, and I will oversee the work." No, he used the first person
plural. As Adeney observes, "In the genuine use of this pro-
noun 'we' there lies the secret of all effective exhortation."[4]
What a wise word to all who serve in places of leadership.

In the second place, Nehemiah *solicited* their cooperation.
"Let us build up the wall of Jerusalem." Again, he made appeal
to all the people. He was fully aware of the fact that he could
not arrange matters with a high hand; he needed their help.

Third, and perhaps most important, Nehemiah *encouraged*
the people with the good word of the king of Persia, prompted
by the hand of God. *"Then I told them of the hand of my God
which was good upon me; as also the king's words that he had
spoken unto me."* Here were the greatest sources of encouragement to proceed with the work.

What was the result of his appeal? It worked! Without a moment's hesitation for committee action—that would have meant
further delay—they replied in unison to his challenge (2:18):
*And they said, Let us rise up and build. So they strengthened
their hands for this good work.*

The date was August 1, 144 B.C.

When considering the success of Nehemiah's appeal, we do
well to note that this man brought the prerequisite for every

work of God: inspiration. He brought no new workers; he brought what was better, new hope. Adeney writes,

> We wait for better men to arise and undertake the tasks that seem to be too great for our strength; we cry for a new race of God-sent heroes to accomplish the Herculean labours before which we faint and fail. But we might ourselves become the better men; nay, assuredly we should become God's heroes, if we would but open our hearts to receive the Spirit by the breath of which the weakest are made strong and the most indolent are fired with a Divine energy. Today, as in the time of Nehemiah, the one supreme need is inspiration.[5]

As the memoir comes to its close, Nehemiah records further evidence of the growing opposition (2:19-20).

> *But when Sanballat the Horonite, and Tobiah the servant, the Ammonite, and Geshem the Arabian, heard it, they laughed us to scorn, and despised us, and said, What is this thing that ye do? will ye rebel against the king? Then answered I them, and said unto them, The God of heaven, he will prosper us; therefore we his servants will arise and build: but ye have no portion, nor right, nor memorial, in Jerusalem.*

Yes, the enemy may ridicule. Hoping to malign our motives, he may insinuate. Let him do his worst! Our Lord faced these things. More than once, adversaries laughed Him to scorn. His early followers were reviled also. But in every instance, a work was to be done, and standing in the shadows was the "God of heaven." With Him as our "public opinion," there is but one thing for us to do: arise and build!

We do not know, but perhaps such a scene was before William P. Merrill when he wrote,

> Rise up, O men of God!
> Have done with lesser things;
> Give heart and soul and mind and strength
> To serve the King of kings.

Rise up, O men of God!
The Church for you doth wait,
Her strength unequal to her task;
Rise up, and make her great!

Lift high the cross of Christ!
Tread where His feet have trod;
As brothers of the Son of Man,
Rise up, O men of God!

So be it!

4

Caution: Men Working

Among the many jewels from the pen of the late Frank W. Boreham is this one: "God is a great believer in putting things down."[1] To this we might add that He puts down even seemingly insignificant things such as lists of *names*. Several passages of Scripture attest to the truth of these words. The book of 2 Samuel (23:8-39) provides us with a catalog of David's mighty men and their deeds of prowess. In the New Testament, Romans 16 supplies several lovely glimpses of some of Paul's spiritual grandchildren, their fellowship, and their service. Here, in chapter three of Nehemiah's memoirs, we mingle with a grand group of men and women hard at work.

What lay behind this extensive directory of names? Two things: Nehemiah's stirring call to arms mentioned earlier in 2:17, *"let us build up the wall of Jerusalem,"* and the people's equally stirring response, *"Let us rise up and build"* (2:18). The chapter before us, Nehemiah 3, identifies "us", and by so doing records for all time what God saw as men worked.

Four important lessons in this major memoir are worth taking to heart and hand.

In the first place, observe that *nearly everyone worked*. We will note the exception in due course. The collective activity of this motley crew was something to behold. Choosing selectively, yet without missing a gate, let us observe the following as recorded by Nehemiah (3:1-32).

Then Eliashib the high priest rose up with his brethren the priests, and they builded the sheep gate. . . . But the fish gate did the sons of Hassenaah build. . . . Moreover the old gate repaired Jehoiada the son of Paseah, and Meshullam the son of Besodeiah. . . . The valley gate repaired Hanun, and the inhabitants of Zanoah. . . . But the dung gate repaired Malchiah the son of Rechab, the ruler of part of Beth-haccerem. . . . the gate of the fountain repaired Shallun the son of Colhozeh, the ruler of part of Mizpah. . . . Moreover the Nethinims dwelt in Ophel, unto the place over against the water gate toward the east, and the tower that lieth out. . . . From above the horse gate repaired the priests. . . . After him repaired also Shemaiah the son of Shechaniah, the keeper of the east gate. . . . After him repaired Malchiah the goldsmith's son unto the place of the Nethinims, and of the merchants, over against the gate Miphkad, and to the going up of the corner. And between the going up of the corner unto the sheep gate repaired the goldsmiths and the merchants.

Consulting a map of the ancient city will make evident that we have circled the wall. We began with the Sheep Gate at the northeast corner and returned to the same gate. This circuit of the wall may be likened to a spiritual journey in the life of the believer. With the encouragement of the sons of Korah in Psalm 48:12-13, let us "walk about Zion" once more, marking well her bulwarks, but this time making appropriate spiritual applications.

The journey begins at the Sheep Gate near the temple area in the northeast section of the city. The name of this gate agrees with its situation. Facing the Mount of Olives, it opened on the Kidron valley and the lonely hills looking toward Jericho. Through this gate the shepherds brought their flocks from the wilderness pasturage. Likely a market was located just inside this gate. Here also the priests performed their endless task. As the Passover season approached, the bleating of sheep would fill the area. Rich associations clustering about that gate would suggest the deep mystery of the sacrificial system and the joy of the paschal redemption of the nation.[2]

For us who believe, "the 'Sheep Gate' has a far more touching significance."[3] Through this gate, where Saint Stephen's Gate now stands, our Lord passed on His journeys between Jerusalem and Bethany. Through the Sheep Gate He went out to Gethsemane on that last awful night, and through the Sheep Gate He probably passed when He was brought back "as a sheep" among her shearers and "as a Lamb" led to the slaughter (Isa 53:7).[4]

The Sheep Gate speaks of the cross. How significant that the work of reconstruction should begin here. And thus it must be. Jessie Pounds was right when she wrote long ago,

> I must needs go home by the way of the cross,
> There's no other way but this;
> I shall ne'er get sight of the Gates of Light,
> If the way of the cross I miss.

Moving counterclockwise, almost due north, we come to the Fish Gate, probably the site of the present-day Damascus Gate. Adeney has suggested that since this gate faced north it would scarcely have been used by traders coming up from the fisheries in the Mediterranean. Rather the Fish Gate must have received the fish supply from the Jordan River and from as far as the Sea of Galilee.[5] However it served, the point of interest for us is the mention of "fish." Remember that the Saviour said to Simon Peter and his brother Andrew, "Follow me, and I will make you fishers of men," (Matt 4:19). In this manner He calls us first to Himself and then to the multitudes as His witnesses.

As we move around the wall in a westerly direction, we come to the Old Gate, perhaps the same gate referred to as the "corner gate" in 2 Kings 14:13 and Jeremiah 31:38. The latter text is a prophetic promise of what we now see in Nehemiah's memoir. One wonders: why was it called the Old Gate? Adeney helps us here: "That a gate should bear such a name would lead

us to think that once gates had not been so numerous as they
were at this time. Yet most probably the 'Old Gate' was really
new, because very little of the original city remained above
ground. But men love to perpetuate memories of the past. Even
what is new in fact may acquire a flavour of age by force of association. The wise reformer will follow the example of Nehemiah in linking the new on to the old, and preserving the vener-
able associations of antiquity wherever these do not hinder
present efficiency."[6]

The spiritual significance of the Old Gate is not easily dis-
cerned. Perhaps Jeremiah's exhortation is of some help here.
He wrote, "Stand ye in the ways, and see, and ask for the old
paths, where is the good way, and walk therein, and ye shall
find rest for your souls" (Jer 6:16). The Scriptures do speak in
one place of the householder who brings forth out of his treas-
ure things new and old.

Moving south we come to the Valley Gate which lay adja-
cent to the valley of Hinnom. Through this gate "the poor
children, victims of the savage Moloch worship, had been led
out to their fate. The name of the gate would be a perpetual
reminder of the darkest passage in the old city's history of sin
and shame."[7] The Valley Gate would rouse regret, not pride.

Of what does this gate speak to us? One is reminded of the
word of the prophet, "To this man will I look, even to him that
is poor and of a contrite spirit, and trembleth at my word" (Isa
66:2). The psalmist adds his own word, "He forgetteth not the
cry of the humble" (Psalm 9:12). How often we need to pause
by this gate, for too easily even Christians tend toward pride
and arrogance.

Hard by the Valley Gate, in the deep south of the wall, we
come to the Dung Gate, through which the refuse of the city
was flung out into the valley below. Even then, people were
aware of the importance of ecology.

Believers must be aware of the need for cleansing in the spiritual sense. After reminding the Corinthians of their close ties

to the Saviour and His promises to them, Paul writes, "Having therefore these promises, dearly beloved, let us cleanse ourselves from all filthiness of the flesh and spirit, perfecting holiness in the fear of God" (2 Cor 7:1).

This brings us to the Gate of the Fountain, named "perhaps after the one natural spring which Jerusalem possesses—now known as the 'Virgin's Fountain,' and near to the pool of Siloam, where the precious water from this spring was stored."[8] More interesting than this gate's identification is its implication. Note that it was after the Dung Gate, where the filth was removed and cleansing experienced, that one came to the Fountain Gate. We see here illustrated those rivers of living waters spoken of by our Lord in John 7:38. Spiritual waters flow from the life of the child of God indwelt by the Holy Spirit and walking in true holiness and godliness.

Moving along eastward, we come next to the Water Gate, where the Nethinim dwelt. The Nethinim, seemingly, appeared in the days of Joshua, and may be identified with the Gibeonites who had been appointed "hewers of wood and drawers of water" for the sanctuary. The incident is preserved for us in Joshua, chapter 9. They were evidently servants to the Levites.

What an instructive picture we have here. "Wherewithal shall a young man cleanse his way?" asked the psalmist. "By taking heed thereto according to thy word" (Psalm 119:9). Note that word of our Lord in John 15:3, "Now ye are clean through the word which I have spoken unto you." The Water Gate is a type of the Word of God. And will you observe that this gate was unique in that it needed no repair. The psalmist was right when he said, "Forever, O LORD, thy word is settled in heaven" (Psalm 119:89).

When I think of that gate I am reminded of some choice words by an unknown author,

> Last eve I paused before a blacksmith's door
> And heard the anvil ring the vesper chime.

And looking in, I saw old hammers on the floor,
  Worn by the beating years of time.

"How many anvils have you had," said I,
  "To wear and batter all these hammers so?"
"Just one," said he, then with a twinkle in his eyes,
  "The anvil wears the hammers out you know."

And so I thought, the anvil of God's word,
  For ages skeptic blows have beat upon.
Yet through the noise of falling blows was heard
  The anvil is unharmed—the hammers gone!

The Horse Gate was the responsibility of some unnamed priests. Through this gate the king's horses were led to their stables. Since the horse was for battle, the Horse Gate suggests the believer's warfare in an alien world. That old warrior, Paul the apostle, describing this warfare in the closing chapter of his Ephesian epistle, identifies with care the various pieces of armor which the soldier of Christ is to wear for battle.

Charles Wesley caught the spirit of that text when he wrote,

Soldiers of Christ, arise,
And put your armor on,
Strong in the strength which God supplies
Through His eternal Son;
Strong in the Lord of hosts,
And in His mighty pow'r,
Who in the strength of Jesus trusts
Is more than Conqueror.

We come now in our circuit to the East Gate, which represents for the believer that great moment for which the church of God waits: the coming of our Lord from heaven to receive His Bride. Many of us can say with the psalmist, "My soul waiteth for the Lord more than they that watch for the morning" (Psalm 130:6).

And so at long last, we come to the gate Miphkad. Little is known about this gate . The word occurs only one other time, in

Ezekiel 43:21: "Thou shalt take the bullock also of the sin offering, and he shall burn it in the appointed place [miphkad] of the house, without the sanctuary." In the light of the expression "the appointed place," it has been suggested that this is the "gate of mustering," or "gate of review." For God's children, this gate seems to forecast that place where all believers will be mustered for the purpose of receiving appropriate rewards. Paul identifies the site as the judgment seat of Christ (2 Cor 5:10).

So ends the journey around Zion's wall.

We remarked at the outset of this memoir that nearly everyone worked. We read in verse 5 of the one painful exception: *"But their nobles put not their necks to the work of the Lord."*

Nehemiah does not supply an explanation for this dereliction of duty. Whether these nobles of Tekoa considered such work below their dignity, or whether some unrevealed breach existed between them and the people, we cannot say.[9] Whatever the cause, it is important we note that God marks the *shirkers* as well as the *workers*. This chapter is not the only instance in Scripture where the Lord gives special attention to the sin of abstention, or negligence. The Bible speaks of the man who, like one building his house on sand, hears the words of Christ but does nothing about them; and of the servant who knew his lord's will but would not do it, and was beaten with many stripes; and of the virgins who failed to fill their vessels with oil and were left behind at the coming of the bridegroom. All these examples, and others, underscore an important but neglected truth: our Lord's most frequent words of condemnation were reserved for what we might call negative evil, that is, the evil of harmless but useless lives.

For the most part, Nehemiah and his people worked, and they worked *together*. Although working together sounds easy, God knew long before this that it would not be easy. When He instructed Israel through Moses, He said, "Ye shall rejoice in all that ye put your hand unto, ye and your households, wherein

the LORD thy God hath blessed thee. Ye shall not do after all
the things that we do here this day, every man whatsoever is
right in his own eyes" (Deut 12:7-8). But the book of Judges
reveals Israel's disregard for this admonition (Judg 17:6; 21:
25).

The project of building the wall had in it all the ingredients
needed for a repetition of those tragic days of the judges: there
were forty-two separate work crews! But the fact remains that
they worked together. No less than thirty-one times we find
the expression *"next to him"* or *"next to them."* How this must
have animated the work. What personal pride could be heard
in such remarks as, "See how fast my work goes on!" Or, "See
how my piece is coming!" Or even, "Now, my sons, gird up
your tunics, and get on with it, or Rephaiah the son of Hur will
get ahead of us." The work progressed in just such a spirit of
coordination.

A third lesson may be gleaned from this memoir. The people
worked at specific tasks and thus demonstrate an important
principle, namely, the strength of the whole wall was in direct
proportion to the strength of each of its parts. Herein lies the
secret to their success in building; each of those forty-two crews
did the work that lay nearest them. This wise arrangement fore-
stalled confusion by discouraging workers from going only to
the best places, or the easiest, or the safest.

Listen to these priceless cameos: *"And next unto them repaired Jedaiah the son of Harumaph, even over against his
house"* (3:10). . . . *"After him repaired Benjamin and Hashub
over against their house"* (3:23). . . . *"After him repaired
Meshullam the son of Berechiah over against his chamber"* (3:
30).

I am especially drawn to the emphasis given Baruch the son
of Zabbai who *"earnestly repaired"* his piece of the wall (3:20).
God not only sees the workmen and takes note of their work,
but He marks the man who does more than is required of him.

As we come to the close of this instructive chapter, one more thing must be cited. Not only did nearly everyone work and work together and work specifically, but each worked on toward the completion of his job. The memoir testifies to that fact. The verb *"repaired"* occurs no less than thirty-four times. These workers did not plan to do something someday. No, each saw his part and did it.

Long live the crews of Nehemiah!

Consider now an incident from modern history. During those dreadful days of the Second World War while Britain was bearing the brunt of Hitler's devastating attacks by sea and air, President Roosevelt sent a personal message to Britain's prime minister, Sir Winston Churchill. In the letter he wrote a verse by Longfellow,

> Thou, too, sail on, O Ship of State!
> Sail on, O Union, strong and great!
> Humanity with all its fears,
> With all its hopes of future years,
> Is hanging breathless on thy fate!

The prime minister reported the incident to the British Commonwealth over the British Broadcasting Company. I shall never forget his words,

> What is the answer that I shall give to this great man in your name? Here is the answer which I shall give to President Roosevelt. Put your confidence in us! Give us your faith and your blessing, and under Providence all will be well. We shall not fail nor falter. We shall not weaken nor tire. Neither the sudden shock of battle, nor the long drawn trial of vigilance and execution will wear us down. Give us the tools and we will finish the job![10]

Thus a great statesman presented a great challenge. What he said, Nehemiah might have cried to his colleagues in their hour of peril. "Give us the tools, and we will finish the job!"

And they did!

5

He Who Would Valiant Be

The literary genius of John Bunyan is a matter of record. His *Pilgrim's Progress* probably has been more widely read than any other book in the English language. What is not known about Bunyan is that he was a hymnist. It is his hymn that provides both the subject and inspiration for our fourth memoir.

> He who would valiant be
> 'Gainst all disaster,
> Let him in constancy,
> Follow the Master.
> There's no discouragement
> Shall make him once relent
> His first avowed intent
> To be a pilgrim.
>
> Whoso beset him round
> With dismal stories,
> Do but themselves confound,
> His strength the more is.
> No foes shall stay his might;
> Though he with giants fight,
> He will make good his right
> To be a pilgrim.
>
> JOHN BUNYAN

As our last study ended, Nehemiah and his band of workers were hard at it. We noted *cooperation* (nearly everyone worked),

· *coordination* (they worked together), *concentration* (they worked specifically), and *consummation* (they executed their work).

It was evident that the construction of the wall was proceeding according to schedule.

Inevitably the enemy attacked again, this time more fiercely. In the second memoir, we referred to the original skirmishes (2: 10, 19). In the present study three distinct attempts were made to stop the work altogether.

The heathen leaders displayed their teeth immediately, and Nehemiah records their initial assault as follows (4:1-3):

> *But it came to pass, that when Sanballat heard that we builded the wall, he was wroth, and took great indignation, and mocked the Jews. And he spake before his brethren and the army of Samaria, and said, What do these feeble Jews? will they fortify themselves? will they sacrifice? will they make an end in a day? will they revive the stones out of the heaps of the rubbish which are burned? Now Tobiah the Ammonite was by him, and he said, Even that which they build, if a fox go up, he shall even break down their stone wall.*

"Dismal stories," Bunyan would call them. And so they may be. But we must not underestimate such an attack upon God's servant and his colleagues, or upon God's children in any generation. *Mockery* (derision, or ridicule) seems to be a major reaction of the men of this world toward those who have chosen to be men of that other world. King Hezekiah faced derision when he attempted reformation after the temple had been neglected and polluted during his father's reign. As the posts, bearing letters from the king, passed from city to city, the Ephraimites and those of Manasseh "laughed them to scorn, and mocked them" (2 Chron 30:10).

But no one faced mockery quite as did our Lord. Anticipating its coming, He forewarned His disciples that He would be delivered up to the Gentiles, *mocked,* and spitefully treated.

And He was. The chief priests mocked Him. Herod mocked
Him! The soldiers mocked Him; they came to Him as He hung
on the cross, and offered Him vinegar.

Consider the experience of the young church, barely born
before the multitudes came together to hear what had happened
at Pentecost. Being unable to explain it, some "mocking said,
These men are full of new wine" (Acts 2:13). Mistaken
though they were in their hasty judgment, in one sense they
were right. These men *were* full of new wine—the wine of the
Holy Spirit.

And these were not alone. There have been others. The
Spirit of God records, "And others had trial of cruel mockings
and scourgings" (Heb 11:36).

Therefore you and I must not be surprised if we face derision
from the enemies of the gospel when we witness for Jesus Christ
in our homes, at our work, in our community, or even in the
church at times.

We learn from 4:7-8 that certain men of the ancient city of
Ashdod now joined the opposition, and the band conspired to
use *force*.

> *But it came to pass, that when Sanballat, and Tobiah, and
> the Arabians, and the Ammonites, and the Ashdodites, heard
> that the walls of Jerusalem were made up, and that the
> breaches began to be stopped, then they were very wroth, and
> conspired all of them together to come and to fight against
> Jerusalem, and to hinder it.*

This desperate expedient would have to be executed in de-
fiance of the Persian king who had granted the Jews permission
to build in the first place. Perhaps these mockers felt they could
always plead that the Jews were mounting a rebellion. Whatever the reasoning, the opposition was formidable.

Strange allies will join ranks against the people of God. Before confronting Jesus of Nazareth, Pilate and Herod were at
each other's throat. But after each found himself unable to

cope with the Son of Man during His trial, they "were made friends together" (Luke 23:12).

This brings us to the third and final attack. In verse 11, Nehemiah tells us, *"And our adversaries said, They shall not know, neither see, till we come in the midst among them, and slay them, and cause the work to cease."*

Thus far, mockery and the threat of force had been encountered. Now Nehemiah and his companions faced *conspiracy*, that ugly undercover activity designed to surprise and work havoc in the assembly. The word was passed along within the enemy's ranks. To complicate the matter, certain Jews, probably among those living in the suburbs, brought Nehemiah repeated warnings. *"They said unto us ten times, From all places whence ye shall return unto us they will be upon you"* (4:12). Conspiracy nurtured in this way by the Jews could only produce anxiety among the workers.

What did Nehemiah do? This memoir directs us to four viable weapons available to all of God's children who face mockery, force, and conspiracy.

In the first place, Nehemiah *prayed.* He heeded the wise counsel of the proverb by answering "not a fool according to his folly" (Prov 26:4). Verse 4 records the content of his intercession.

> *Hear, O our God; for we are despised: and turn their reproach upon their own head, and give them for a prey in the land of captivity: and cover not their iniquity, and let not their sin be blotted out from before thee: for they have provoked thee to anger before the builders.*

Before considering a troublesome matter in this prayer, let us say this much about it: Nehemiah evidently considered prayer his first line of defense; Adeney says it was his sheet anchor.[1] Herein is a timeless lesson. In the face of enemy attack, we are in danger of resorting to natural impatience and the energy of the flesh. We forget Paul's sage counsel to the

Corinthian church and to us "For though we live in the world, we do not wage war as the world does. The weapons we fight with are not the weapons of the world. On the contrary, they have divine power to tear down strongholds" (2 Cor 10:3-4 NIV).

Hezekiah knew this. When Rab-shakeh, commander of Sennacherib's Assyrian army threatened Hezekiah and his people, that godly king "went up into the house of the LORD, and spread it before the LORD. . . . And . . . *prayed*" (2 Kings 19:14-15). In the presence of his enemies, Nehemiah likewise laid hold of this unfailing source of strength: *"Hear, O our God; for we are despised."*

Nehemiah's splendid example of personal prayer appears to have been contagious. *"We made our prayer unto our God"* (4:9) suggests that as their leader led them in prayer, the people caught his spirit of devotion and were moved to join him in united and earnest intercession.

But now, what are we to say about Nehemiah's cursing his enemies? Rather than forgiving them, he actually besought the Lord that He would not forgive. What about such a maledictory spirit? Two things need to be remembered. In the first place, Nehemiah believed that God and the people of God are inseparable. To despise the Jews was to despise Jehovah. Thus the ground upon which Nehemiah urges his petition is: *"They have provoked thee to anger before the builders"* (4:5). Second, this prayer must be understood in the context of the dispensation in which it appears. A. F. Kirkpatrick, in *The Book of Psalms,* has summarized the matter as well as anyone. He says of the imprecatory psalms (e.g., 58, 59, 69, 83, 109, 137) and Nehemiah's prayer, "They must be viewed as belonging to the dispensation of the Old Testament; they must be estimated from the standpoint of the Law, which was based upon the rule of retaliation, and not the Gospel, which is animated by the principle of love; they belong to the spirit of Elijah, not of

Christ; they use the language of the age which was taught to love its neighbour and hate its enemy."[2]

All such utterances, then, belong to the age in which the martyr's dying prayer was not, "Lord, lay not this sin to their charge" (Acts 7:60), but rather, "May the LORD see this and exact the penalty" (2 Chron 24:22, NEB).* Nehemiah was of that breed. He was a great and good man, but he was not an "Old Testament Christ."

So Nehemiah and the people *prayed,* but as they continued building, they employed a second means to foil the opposition (4:9): *"Nevertheless we made our prayer unto our God, and set a watch against them day and night, because of them."*

At this point, especially after the remarkable display of dependence upon the Lord as witnessed in prayer, we might be inclined to ask, Was not prayer sufficient; why this setting of a watch and the arming with weapons if they trusted God? Dr. Sidlow Baxter replies,

> It was because Nehemiah was not the fanatic to blunder into the delusion that faith is presumption. There are situations in which we can do absolutely nothing for ourselves, and then it is perfectly right to trust God to do absolutely everything; but in other cases, where there are reasonable precautions which we ourselves can take, we ought to take them. . . . Petition without precaution is presumption.[3]

Thus setting a watch became the Jews' second means of foiling the enemy. Our Lord Himself, anticipating the opposition His disciples would face, said "Watch and pray, that ye enter not into temptation" (Matt 26:41). Paul, that old warrior of many a spiritual skirmish, when he wrote to the church at Colosse said, "Continue in prayer, and watch in the same" (Col 4:2).

Cromwell was right, then, when he said, "Trust in God, and keep your powder dry!"

*New English Bible.

Therefore *watch!*

The memoir moves on to provide us with a third weapon for meeting the enemy. To prayer and watchfulness we must add *encouragement* (4:14).

> *And I looked, and rose up, and said unto the nobles, and to the rulers, and to the rest of the people, Be not ye afraid of them: remember the Lord, which is great and terrible, and fight for your brethren, your sons, and your daughters, your wives, and your houses.*

The words, *"I looked, and rose up"* are intriguing. Was this one of those occasions when Nehemiah shot an arrow heavenward before speaking to the people? If so, he would be emulated by another great leader, Stonewall Jackson, general of the armies of the South. On the battlefield, Jackson would frequently look up, as if imploring wisdom before giving an order to his men. In any case, with stirring words Nehemiah called his people to courage under fire: *"Remember the Lord."*

Those of us who have lived through the agonizing years of the Second World War will not forget the cry that went up following the Japanese attack, "Remember Pearl Harbor!" But in this word of Nehemiah, we have an even greater antidote for faintheartedness. When we apprehend the presence and power of God by faith and measure our foes by what He is, we will have courage enough to say, "If God be for us, who can be against us" (Rom 8:31).

Nehemiah added the challenge, *"Fight for your brethren, your sons, and your daughters, your wives, and your houses"* (4:14). Make no mistake about it; the Jews were engaged in no sham battle. They were fighting for their lives. The brotherhood of the race (*"brethren"*), the blessings of family and home (*"sons and daughters"*), the ties of personal affection (*"wives"*), and cherished inheritances (*"houses"*) were at stake. They must fight or perish.

The fourth and final piece of strategy employed against the

enemy was the use of *arms*. The memoir is detailed at this point; we shall note only verse 17:

> *They which builded on the wall, and they that bare burdens, with those that laded, every one with one of his hands wrought in the work, and with the other hand held a weapon.*

Being forewarned, they were forearmed. Every man who built also bore arms. The sword and trowel went together. On the seal of a certain missionary society is engraved an ox standing between a plough and an altar. Over the scene this motto appears: "Ready for Either." So it was with these patriots of Zion; they were ready for labor or for sacrifice.

We should not be surprised therefore that Nehemiah tells us in verse 15,

> *And it came to pass, when our enemies heard that it was known unto us, and God had brought their counsel to nought, that we returned all of us to the wall, every one unto his work.*

Not a blow was struck. Fortunately for the enemy, this was so. Had they ventured to attack at any point along the wall, the good governor would have seen them and sounded the trumpet. Picked men, running to meet the foe, would have been joined in short order by the armed builders. The Jews would have engaged the attackers on every side and cut them to pieces. So they kept on praying, kept on watching and kept on working.

Following the collapse of France during those grim days of the Second Word War, naturally the question asked was, Will Britain surrender too? At that critical moment Sir Winston Churchill rose to the occasion. Addressing the House of Commons on June 18, 1940, Mr. Churchill acknowledged that the battle of France was over. He went on to say,

> I expect that the battle of Britain is about to begin. Upon this battle depends the survival of Christian civilization. Upon it depends our own British life, and the long continuity of our

institutions and our Empire. The whole fury and might of the enemy must very soon be turned on us. Hitler knows that he will have to break us in this island or lose the war. If we stand up to him, all Europe may be free and the life of the world may move forward into broad sunlit uplands. But if we fail, then the whole world, including the United States, including all that we have known and cared for, will sink into the abyss of a new Dark Age, made more sinister, and perhaps more protracted, by the lights of perverted science. Let us therefore brace ourselves to our duties, and so bear ourselves that, if the British Empire and its Commonwealth last for a thousand years, men will still say, "This was their finest hour."[4]

When those words were spoken, they were only words. But when victory finally came, they had been forged into flesh and blood. It was Britain's finest hour!

So it was that Nehemiah saw issues, provided inspiration, and challenged a nation of despised Jews to achieve victory. In that setting, and nearing the close of the memoir, he writes very simply: *"So we labored in the work"* (4:21).

6

Union Don'ts and Dos

The fifth memoir opens with what one commentator calls "a shock of pain." With characteristic candor, Nehemiah identifies a new and sinister trouble (5:1). *"And there was a great cry of the people and of their wives against their brethren the Jews."*

What was the occasion for this shock of pain which drove Nehemiah to the mercy seat? The words, *"this people,"* supply the answer (5:19). Until now, the opposition by and large had come from that crowd of hooligans, Sanballat and Company. True, there had been a minor ripple when the men of Judah said to Nehemiah, *"The strength of the bearers of burdens is decayed, and there is much rubbish; so that we are not able to build the wall"* (4:10). But that was minor compared with what was happening now: Discord appeared *within* the family; something was taking place inside Israel which threatened her life and witness.

It is generally agreed that the new problem was a family affair involving *"the people and their wives,"* that is, the poor majority, and *"their brethren the Jews,"* the rich minority. The specifics of their contention will concern us later. For now, let us concentrate on the combatants, and from them seek to learn the lesson that the Spirit of God would teach us.

Who were *"this people"*? They were brethren. Together they formed that feeble remnant which had responded earlier to the appeals of Zerubbabel and Ezra and, more recently of Nehemiah, to return to the land of their fathers in a common cause. Alas, how unlike brethren they were acting just now, despite the reproof of the prophet Malachi, Nehemiah's contemporary: "Have we not all one father? hath not one God created us? why do we deal treacherously every man against his brother, by profaning the covenant of our fathers?" (Mal 2:10).

To give the widest possible understanding of the place of the believer in the family of God, particularly by the New Testament definition, let us consider the *family name*. We shall mention several scriptural terms in what would seem to be their logical sequence.

1. *The children of God.* This is the apostle John's special name for the believer. It occurs in the familiar text, John 1:12, where the *New American Standard Bible* correctly translates the term "sons" as "children." Except for Revelation 21:7, which is really a quotation, John does not use "sons" to describe the relationship of believers to God. He regards their position to be the result of a new life. To John, the relationship is of *nature,* not adoption as in the writings of Paul.

2. *Sons.* This term is Pauline and is found in such texts as Galatians 4:4-5, where the apostle says, "God sent forth His Son, made of a woman, made under the law, to redeem them that were under the law, that we might receive the adoption of sons." Paul regards the believer's relationship from the legal standpoint and therefore as a matter of son-placing and heirship.

3. *Disciples.* This term occurs frequently in the gospels and the book of the Acts. (*Disciple* is best understood by the term *learner,* that is, one who professes to have learned certain principles from someone else and who holds them on the authority of the other person. The expression was applied in a special sense to the twelve.)

4. *Friends.* Our Lord favored this term when discoursing with His own. John 15:13-15 is an example. "Ye are my

friends. . . . I have called you friends; for all things that I
have heard of my Father I have made known unto you"
suggest intimacy and communion with Him.

How accurately Fanny Crosby catches this thought in
her familiar hymn "I am Thine, O Lord."

> O the pure delight of a single hour
> That before Thy throne I spend,
> When I kneel in prayer, and with Thee, my God,
> I commune as friend with friend.

5. *Servants.* While this term found its way into the vocabulary
   of our Lord on occasion, it appears more often in the Acts
   of the Apostles and the epistles. In Acts 4:29, we hear the
   cry of the company of the committed as they pray, "And
   now, Lord, behold their threatenings: and grant unto thy
   servants, that with all boldness they may speak thy word."
   "Servant" in the Bible is the familiar word for *bondman.*

6. *Christians.* Not until we reach the new community of believers at Antioch of Syria where Paul and Barnabas ministered for some twelve months, do we come upon this
   now common word for the believer in Jesus Christ. In Acts
   11:26 we read, "And the disciples were called Christians
   first in Antioch."

7. *Saints.* However reluctant some may be to use this term
   in reference to God's children, still it appears again and
   again in Scripture. And rightly so. As Merrill Unger writes,
   "All the saved of the N.T. era are saints . . . by virtue of
   their *position* 'in Christ.' "[1] Nowhere is this more evident
   than in Paul's salutation to the Corinthians. For all their
   faults, he still speaks to them in his greeting as those "that
   are sanctified in Christ Jesus, called to be saints." (1 Cor
   1:2).

After noting all these, we come to the question that our present memoir raises: what one term really touches the heart of
our family relationship? It is the term *brethren.* From such

texts as Acts 9:30 and 1 Corinthians 5:11; 11:2, it would seem
this was the name by which the early converts were known best
until they were called Christians at Antioch. Even then, the
term brethren found its way into their conversation. Perhaps
the Lord Himself gave that term its peculiar value, for we are
told in the epistle to the Hebrews, "For both he that sanctifieth
and they who are sanctified are all of one: for which cause he
is not ashamed to call them brethren" (2:11).

Here, then, is the *family name*.

(This term *brethren* occurs five times in the chapter before us,)
and its mention brought Nehemiah to the boiling point when
he learned what the brethren were doing to each other. Note
verse 6: *"And I was very angry when I heard their cry and these
words."*

This brings us to a second matter: the *family shame*. The
memoir details the problem as follows (5:2-7).

> *For there were that said, We, our sons, and our daughters,
> are many: therefore we take up corn for them, that we may eat,
> and live. Some also there were that said, We have mortgaged
> our lands, vineyards, and houses, that we might buy corn, be-
> cause of the dearth. There were also that said, We have bor-
> rowed money for the king's tribute, and that upon our lands
> and vineyards. Yet now our flesh is as the flesh of our breth-
> ren, our children as their children: and, lo, we bring into bond-
> age our sons and our daughters to be servants, and some of
> our daughters are brought unto bondage already: neither is it
> in our power to redeem them; for other men have our lands
> and vineyards.*

Here we get the specifics of the problem which caused Nehemiah both anger and grief. While not ignoring the deeper issues, we must not close our eyes to the practical predicament
which precipitated this new crisis. To begin with, there was the
obvious problem of a *population explosion*. Complained the
brethren, *"We, our sons, and our daughters, are many."* The
number of the poor in comparison with the rich was probably

disproportionately large. Moreover, because of the heavy demands pressed upon the people in their work of restoring the wall, *agricultural pursuits*, which would secure adequate food supplies, were neglected. And finally, former governors had impoverished the populace by excessive *taxation* to the crown. *"We have borrowed money for the king's tribute,"* they cried.

It was a familiar set of social evils. To make matters worse, some within the ranks were taking advantage of the situation and charging exorbitant interest—as much as 12 percent. Furthermore, mortgages were made, and in some cases children were sold, to pay debts. Most shocking was the fact that the extortioners were Jews making profit at the expense of their own. As Baxter says, "It was a plague of greed."

The men of the world might argue here: What was wrong with this? Were these loan sharks not being shrewd? The world might excuse their actions, but to Nehemiah, the servant of the Lord, such practices were clearly wrong. This conviction surfaces in verses 7-10, where Nehemiah cries out in a great assembly,

> *Then I consulted with myself, and I rebuked the nobles, and the rulers, and said unto them, Ye exact usury, every one of his brother. And I set a great assembly against them. And I said unto them, We after our ability have redeemed our brethren the Jews, which were sold unto the heathen; and will ye even sell your brethren? or shall they be sold unto us? Then held they their peace, and found nothing to answer. Also I said, It is not good that ye do: ought ye not to walk in the fear of our God because of the reproach of the heathen our enemies? I likewise, and my brethren, and my servants, might exact of them money and corn: I pray you, let us leave off this usury.*

In passing, observe the remark of Nehemiah in verse 7, *"Then I consulted with myself."* Because the leaders with whom he might have taken counsel were themselves the chief offenders in this internal problem, they were of no help to Nehemiah. Thus he was cast upon God and his own counsel for the answer.

Sometimes when there has been departure from the ways of the
Lord, and as a result the authority of the Word of God has been
obscured, the man of God must act alone. Having consulted
with Him in the sanctuary, God's servant was ready now to
· administer a firm and faithful rebuke.

What means does he employ to do this? The answer is supplied in the text. First, Nehemiah reminded the people that
what they had done was not good in the light of the fear of God.
This precise phrase "in the fear of our God" does not appear
elsewhere in the Old Testament. It seems to condense the
thought in Deuteronomy 10:12, "And now, Israel, what doth
the LORD require of thee, but to fear the LORD thy God, to walk
in all his ways, and to love him, and to serve the LORD thy God
with all thy heart and with all thy soul."

Proper fear of God, reverence for Him, will result in obedience to the revealed Word of God. This was the deeper issue involved in their conduct, an issue they had chosen to ignore.
But Nehemiah remembered it. He recalled that, as far back as
Leviticus, God had said to Israel through Moses,

> And if thy brother be waxen poor, and fallen in decay with
> thee; thou shalt relieve him: yea, though he be a stranger, or
> a sojourner; that he may live with thee. Take thou no usury
> of him, or increase: but fear thy God; that thy brother may
> live with thee. Thou shalt not give him thy money upon usury,
> nor lend him thy victuals for increase. . . . For they are my
> servants, which I brought forth out of the land of Egypt: they
> shall not be sold as bondmen (Lev 25:35-37, 42).

That command is repeated twice in Deuteronomy. In chapter 15:8, the Lord adds this touching word with regard to the
poor brother, "Thou shalt open thine hand wide unto him, and
shalt surely lend him sufficient for his need, in that which he
wanteth." In chapter 23, He goes beyond this to offer a promise
to those who show concern for their own: "That the LORD thy
God may bless thee in all that thou settest thine hand to in the
land whither thou goest to possess it" (Deut 23:20).

Oppression of one another for the sake of personal gain was a clear violation of the precepts of Scripture. "What did it amount to?" asks Edward Dennett in his exposition on Nehemiah.

> Simply the adoption of human thoughts instead of God's, of worldly usages and practices instead of those prescribed in the Scriptures. In a word, these Jews walked as men, and as men who hastened to be rich at the expense of their brethren! And is this sin unknown in the church of God? Nay, do not the usages of society and the maxims of the world often force themselves among Christians, and regulate their mutual relationships? Let our own consciences answer the question in the presence of God, and we shall soon discover if the sin of these Jews has its counterpart to-day amongst the Lord's people.[2]

God's servant then employed a second means of rebuke. After reminding the people that they were walking in deliberate disobedience to the Word of God, he also reminded them that such conduct brought discredit to God before the nations around them. *"It is not good that ye do . . . because of the reproach of the heathen our enemies,"* he cried. The honor of God was dear to Nehemiah's heart, and he was grieved to think that the conduct of the people of Israel should provide an occasion for reproach among the enemy. They claimed, and rightly so, to be the chosen people of Jehovah, and as such to be separated from all other peoples for His service. But alas, if in their walk they resembled the nations, what of their profession? They were publicly profaning the holy name by which they were called.

We are reminded here of the New Testament counterpart to this sad state of affairs in Israel. In his Corinthian letter, Paul raises the issue of believers going to law with fellow believers before the unsaved. Without any hesitation, the apostle administers a strong rebuke: "Dare any of you, having a matter against another, go to law before the unjust, and not before the saints?

. . . I speak to your shame. Is it so, that there is not a wise man
among you? no, not one that shall be able to judge between his
brethren?" (1 Cor 6:1, 5). That was a strong word from Paul's
pen, but he knew the Lord's own method for settling such differences (Matt 18:15-17), and he did not hesitate to rebuke
them. As Roy Laurin aptly puts it: "to take the differences of
Christians before the world and say, in substance, we have
lofty doctrines but we have neither the grace to get along, nor
the government to get together" is to demean the gospel.[3]

Of course this delights Satan and other enemies of the gospel.
If they can get the saints in Corinth—or Chicago—to act like
Corinthians instead of Christians, they have won a major vic-
tory and hindered our witness to the world.

Nehemiah saw this.

Having spoken to the people of their disobedience to the
Word of God, having reminded them that such disobedience
brings discredit to God and His cause before the heathen, Nehemiah closed his appeal with a personal word (5:10). It was a
word based upon example: his own character and conduct.
While others before him had misused their privileges of leadership, Nehemiah could testify (5:14-16),

> *Moreover from the time that I was appointed to be their*
> *governor in the land of Judah, from the twentieth year even*
> *unto the two and thirtieth year of Artaxerxes the king, that is,*
> *twelve years, I and my brethren have not eaten the bread of the*
> *governor. But the former governors that had been before me*
> *were chargeable unto the people, and had taken of them bread*
> *and wine, beside forty shekels of silver; yea, even their servants*
> *bare rule over the people: but so did not I, because of the fear*
> *of God. Yea, also I continued in the work of this wall, neither*
> *bought we any land: and all my servants were gathered thither*
> *unto the work.*

In essence, Nehemiah could say that for twelve years he had
given a demonstration of honest administration, and was there-

fore in a position to rebuke them for their unworthy conduct. As another has noted, "Happy is the man who has not lost his influence for righteous living."

This man by his own sermon of personal example could now call his people to action with an appeal which was both calm and convincing (5:10-11):

> *I pray you, let us leave off this usury. Restore, I pray you, to them, even this day, their lands, their vineyards, their olive-yards, and their houses, also the hundredth part of the money, and of the corn, the wine, and the oil, that ye exact of them.*

Observe that Nehemiah took the position of identification with his people in their defection. By using the words *"let us,"* he confessed that he was one with them before God. He sought in a spirit of meekness to effect their restoration.

The thrust found its mark (5:12). *"Then said they, We will restore them, and will require nothing of them; so will we do as thou sayest."*

This brings us, then, to the final phase of this memoir's movement: the *family frame.* Nehemiah's candid call to restoration found an immediate response. *"We will restore"* implies a restitution of fields, vineyards, oliveyards, and houses seized in default of payment. Lest they should forget their promise, Nehemiah summoned the priests and bound them to their oath to administer adjudication between debtor and creditor. Then he gave visual solemnity to the whole transaction (5:13): *"Also I shook my lap, and said, So God shake out every man from his house, and from his labour, that performeth not this promise, even thus be he shaken out, and emptied."*

Obviously this was a symbolical gesture to emphasize Nehemiah's call to restoration. By a symbolic act he was following the example of some of the ancient prophets when they denounced those who would not keep the commandments exacted of them. Here, it amounted to a threat of confiscation and excommunication if their pledge were not heeded.

But neither was necessary. The hearts of the people were conformed to their promise. When the appeal to restore was given, the whole congregation replied, *"We will restore . . . so will we do as thou sayest,"* after which they pronounced their *"Amen"* in unison and praised the Lord. A spirit of revival had begun.

I recall an incident which occurred in one of my pastorates many years ago. As was my custom, I met with the choir for prayer before proceeding to the sanctuary. As the last of the men made their way out, a small girl, probably all of six, came into the room. It was her Sunday school classroom, and she knew why she had come. Without hesitation, and ignoring me for the moment, she went straight to a table and opened the drawer. Then from her purse she took a crayon and carefully put it back where it belonged. Closing the drawer and turning to leave, she took a quick look in my direction, smiled, and left without a word.

I felt I understood what she was doing. But I thought of the application of that simple incident. If only all of God's children would behave so specifically and promptly, what a different church the church of God would be. Restoration brings revival.

7

No Time for a Coffee Break

John Newton's beloved hymn "Amazing Grace" has a fitting frame for our sixth memoir. In the third verse he wrote,

> Through many dangers, toils and snares,
> I have already come;
> 'Tis grace hath brought me safe thus far,
> And grace will lead me home.

Nehemiah would have liked that verse, for dangers, toils, and snares there had been, and the end was not yet. The enemies had tried mockery and threats bordering on massacre in the dark but thus far had failed in every attempt on the life of God's servant. All the while, the wall was being raised around the ancient city until not a breach remained, save for the doors which had not yet been hung at the gates. The main work was done; the fortification of Jerusalem had proceeded so far by now that it was hopeless for the enemy to attempt to hinder it by violence. He must change his tactics. What he could not do by *force* he must now attempt by *fraud* involving craft and guile. In reality, this was a confession of failure, but intrigue was all that was left.

We are reminded of two basic weapons in Satan's demonic arsenal. There is the roaring lion weapon of which Peter speaks. "Be sober, be vigilant; because your adversary the devil, as a roaring lion, walketh about, seeking whom he may devour" (1 Pet 5:8). But having failed here, the enemy, hoping to bring the work of God to nought, can change himself into an

angel of light. Paul warns us: "Satan himself is transformed
into an angel of light. Therefore it is no great thing if his ministers also be transformed" (2 Cor 11:14-15).

Returning to the present memoir, we note that while the
internal problems which confronted the little Jewish community
were resolved without blighting the tie that bound the brethren
together, the threat from *without* revived. This time it took on
new and more sinister forms.

Let us read Nehemiah's own account of this new activity of
the adversary (6:1-4).

> *Now it came to pass, when Sanballat, and Tobiah, and
> Geshem the Arabian, and the rest of our enemies, heard that
> I had builded the wall, and that there was no breach left there-
> in; (though at that time I had not set up the doors upon the
> gates;) that Sanballat and Geshem sent unto me, saying, Come,
> let us meet together in some one of the villages in the plain of
> Ono. But they thought to do me mischief. And I sent mes-
> sengers unto them, saying, I am doing a great work, so that I
> cannot come down: why should the work cease, whilst I leave
> it, and come down to you? Yet they sent unto me four times
> after this sort; and I answered them after the same manner.*

On the face of it, the invitation of the enemy appeared to be
a friendly gesture to attend a conference on personnel and man-
agement. It was a formal invitation to Nehemiah to meet them
in a village some twenty miles from Jerusalem to establish
détente of sorts. The name of the city where the conference was
proposed was Ono, a city which constituted the valley of crafts-
men (11:35). How clever of Sanballat and his stooges.

"Sorry schemers!" writes Charles Reade. "Fancy these shal-
low traitors sending this to an Oriental statesman!—a bare hook
without a bait."[1] No wonder then that the conference trick
failed miserably. This Israelite in whom was no guile made
reply in words which revealed his astonishing discernment of
their intentions. He parried their proposals with cool contempt
(6:3).

And I sent messengers unto them, saying, I am doing a great work, so that I cannot come down: why should the work cease, whilst I leave it, and come down to you?

Nehemiah sensed at once that even if his personal safety were not endangered by such a meeting as Sanballat proposed, to leave the work now might give the people an excuse to plead for time off to tend to other matters. Thus they would provide the enemy with an opportunity to steal into the city through the unfinished gates. Accordingly, Nehemiah determined that nothing would turn him aside from his work. Neither would he venture into the enemy's net, from whence he would never again return to Jerusalem. The last sentence of verse 2 seems to suggest that the invitation was meant to decoy him to his death.

So he gave a definitive negative reply: *"I am doing a great work, so that I cannot come down."* There was no conceit in that word. It was true. To leave Jerusalem for one of the villages of Benjamin would mean leaving the work to which God had called him so distinctly when back in the palace in Persia. To leave would indeed be a "come down," and despite their fourfold renewal of the invitation, his answer was the same each time. The enemy may have thought that that which had conquered Samson would conquer Nehemiah. But like a rock, Nehemiah stood fast. "This one thing I do," he said in effect. "I have a wall to finish; finish I must; finish I will!"

So it came to pass that the first snare did not succeed.

Irritated by such granitelike contempt and refusal to respond to their conference trick, the enemies resorted to scandal (6: 5-7).

Then sent Sanballat his servant unto me in like manner the fifth time with an open letter in his hand; wherein was written, It is reported among the heathen, and Gashmu saith it, that thou and the Jews think to rebel: for which cause thou buildest the wall, that thou mayest be their king, according to these words. And thou hast also appointed prophets to preach of thee at Jerusalem, saying, There is a king in Judah: and now

shall it be reported to the king according to these words. Come
now therefore, and let us take counsel together.

Here was a significant alteration in enemy tactics. This time
they sent Nehemiah a postcard, a piece of mail which anyone
could read if he felt like doing so. This seems to be the clear
meaning of the expression *"an open letter."* Ordinarily, such a
letter was sent rolled up in a small silk bag. This custom assured
that its contents would be private and was a courtesy to the re-
cipient of the letter. Of course Sanballat and his band of miscre-
ants had no intention of showing Nehemiah consideration. The
message and the manner in which it was delivered made it quite
certain that other eyes would see its contents. It was a black-
mail attempt of the most vicious kind.

Judging from the charges, the postcard must have been the
giant-sized variety. Three allegations were made. First, the
sender spoke of rebellion—and even suggested a witness, Gashmu, the Arabian. Then he insinuated that Nehemiah was building the wall in order to make himself king. Finally, he inti-
mated that the good governor had bribed prophets to say that
there was a king in Jerusalem.

We must not overlook the fact that there was an element of
truth in that last charge. A child of the covenant in Israel could
not forget that all the nation's hopes were centered in the promised Messiah. It is entirely possible that Nehemiah did attempt,
through the ministry of prophets like Haggai, Zechariah and
Malachi, to revive flagging aspirations for the coming Kingdom.
The craft of Satan is plainly in view in Sanballat's letter.

There was reason for alarm. No doubt Nehemiah, during his
presence at the Persian court, had witnessed instances of the
fatal consequences of displeasing the king. More than once
the monarch's mind had been poisoned, and a good work in
Judah aborted. Nehemiah had cause to wonder now whether
he could rely on his sovereign's favor when he was far from the
royal court and unable to answer for himself the barbs of those

lying tongues. Plainly it was not a comfortable situation. And
Sanballat knew it. Now, he felt certain, Nehemiah would come
to terms with him and consent to a meeting.

But once more, God's servant met the charges with his usual
candor and firmness (6:8-9).

> *Then I sent unto him, saying, There are no such things done
> as thou sayest, but thou feignest them out of thine own heart.
> For they all made us afraid, saying, Their hands shall be weak-
> ened from the work, that it be not done. Now therefore, O
> God, strengthen my hands.*

Some have suggested that Nehemiah's reply was also an open
letter! Perhaps, to conserve paper, the good man wrote his
answer on the original postcard and sent it on its way. In any
event, we mark two things in his reply. To the enemy, his answer was both brief and restrained. Nehemiah knew what he
knew. He knew that his coming to Jerusalem was for the sole
purpose of building a wall, not to establish an empire. In the
words of another, Nehemiah "retired behind the brazen wall of
conscious integrity."[2]

To Jehovah, his answer was in the form of a prayer, *"Now
therefore, O God, strengthen my hands."* The enemy had said,
"Their hands shall be weakened." So Nehemiah prayed for
strong hands. How simple. How definite. He was heroic in
the world before men, but in the secret place Nehemiah knew
his real human weakness. Thus, with unashamed honesty, he
reminded the Lord of the enemy's intentions and asked for
strong hands.

That was prayer with a purpose. It is the kind of prayer we
need. Too often we are vague as the dear brother who, at the
midweek service, always prayed, "O God, loose us from the cob-
webs of our sins." A young man who also attended the prayer
service took note of the repetitious remark. To his youthful
thinking it really missed the mark. On one occasion, when the

old man finished and sat down, the youth ventured his own postscript, "O Lord, kill the spider!"

That was Nehemiah. By sheer honesty he was delivered from the snare of scandal.

The third trap laid for our friend was perhaps the most dangerous trap of all. Since it was apparent that the enemy could not lure him outside the wall, they would attack him within the city. In order to expedite their new attack, they bribed Shemaiah, one of Nehemiah's own kinsmen within the city of Jerusalem, to meet with him in the temple under the pretense that his life was in danger. The memorandum as recorded by Nehemiah reads (6:10),

> *Afterward I came unto the house of Shemaiah the son of Delaiah the son of Mehetabeel, who was shut up; and he said, Let us meet together in the house of God, within the temple, and let us shut the doors of the temple: for they will come to slay thee; yea, in the night will they come to slay thee.*

In a word, what was the intent of this treachery? To get Nehemiah occupied with Nehemiah. If his enemies had succeeded in getting this courageous man to give way at last to fear for his life, what a victory it would have been for them. If he had succumbed, what a defeat for Nehemiah who, in the eyes of his countrymen, was Mr. Single-heart personified.[3]

Once again Nehemiah saw through their treacherous trap. He was neither blinded by self-interest nor overawed by false prophets.[4] Listen to his response (6:11-14).

> *And I said, Should such a man as I flee? and who is there, that, being as I am, would go into the temple to save his life? I will not go in. And, lo, I perceived that God had not sent him; but that he pronounced this prophecy against me: for Tobiah and Sanballat had hired him. Therefore was he hired, that I should be afraid, and do so, and sin, and that they might have matter for an evil report, that they might reproach me. My God, think thou upon Tobiah and Sanballat according to these*

*their works, and on the prophetess Noadiah, and the rest of
the prophets, that would have put me in fear.*

"*I will not go in.*" Talk of a declaration like the sound of a
trumpet! In five words, Nehemiah affirmed his conviction that
the house of God was not meant to be a hiding place from the
harsh and sometimes harmful assaults of the world, but rather
a haven where strength and vision are renewed so that the fight
may be fought to the finish. He feared man little because he
feared God much.

J. Sidlow Baxter, writing from his own honorable and considerable pastoral experience, puts this particular problem in contemporary perspective when he writes,

> It seems an awful thing to say, yet it is true, that there are
> betrayers like Shemaiah and Noadiah . . . in most Christian
> congregations to-day—men and women who have professed
> conversion to Christ, who share in the fellowship and labours
> of the saints, who nevertheless seem to find . . . cruel pleasure
> in the fall of a Christian leader. To his face they are friendly,
> fussy, saintly, but behind his back they are mischiefmakers.
> They profess loyalty and concern, yet if he slips or falls they
> love to gossip it among the brethren or talk it round the town.
> Oh, what heart-pangs such disloyal brethren give to Christian
> ministers, pastors, superintendents, and leaders! They are
> Tobiah's Quislings, Satan's fifth-columnists.[5]

This leads us to a general question: What interest have we in
these machinations against Nehemiah? In the language of
Paul, great warrior of New Testament cast, "Much every way!"
The work at Jerusalem may be regarded as symbolic of the
work of grace with its difficulties, its hindrances, its snares until
the work is done. The Christian experience is also a race which
we must run with patience, laying aside every weight and the
sin which so easily besets, if we would win the prize. It is a warfare with the world, the flesh, and the devil, and we need the
whole armor of God, every piece in place, if we would obtain

the victory and receive the plaudit of our Lord, "Well done, good and faithful servant . . . enter thou into the joy of thy Lord" (Matt 25:23).

Two brief but significant postscripts complete the memoir. In verse 15, Nehemiah records in his diary. *"So the wall was finished in the twenty and fifth day of the month Elul, in fifty and two days."*

There is little doubt that the wall was rough-hewn at this time. Whatever its condition, it was a remarkable feat when we consider the strategems of the enemy within and without, all of which took their toll of time from the actual construction. These things aside, Nehemiah acknowledged that the task was completed by something more than human hands. Even the enemy knew this. Nehemiah writes (6:16),

> *And it came to pass, that when all our enemies heard thereof, and all the heathen that were about us saw these things, they were much cast down in their own eyes: for they perceived that this work was wrought of our God.*

No, the completed wall was not to be explained in terms of human ability alone; God was working His plan by working His people.

The second postscript involves one more insidious snare. Verses 17-19 set the scene for us, and tell what developed.

> *Moreover in those days the nobles of Judah sent many letters unto Tobiah, and the letters of Tobiah came unto them. For there were many in Judah sworn unto him, because he was the son in law of Shechaniah the son of Arah; and his son Johanan had taken the daughter of Meshullam the son of Berechiah. Also they reported his good deeds before me, and uttered my words to him. And Tobiah sent letters to put me in fear.*

What strange affairs can befall the children of men—even the children of God! In the case before us, leading Jewish families were intermarrying with foreigners. Tobiah was playing a little game of his own; he had married a Jewess, and his son had followed his example. To add to the problem, they were corresponding with one another; that is, they were hobnobbing by mail. The constant stream of letters between Tobiah and the sympathizing leaders in Judah could not but create suspicion in the mind of Nehemiah. Now he knew that he had men about him whose confidence he could no longer trust. Whatever the motive of Tobiah and his colleagues, such compromise proved to be but one more snare for God's servant, and another reminder that his trust must rest in God alone. "The stoutest walls will not protect from treason within the ramparts."

So it was that Nehemiah sent up his simple prayer for help, *"My God, think thou upon Tobiah."*

The life and ministry of George Heath must remain in obscurity until the coming again of our Lord. But his hymn provides the substance for gathering together the fragments of the chapter now complete. Wrote Heath,

> My soul be on thy guard;
> Ten thousand foes arise;
> The hosts of sin are pressing hard
> To draw thee from the skies.
>
> O watch and fight and pray;
> The battle ne'er give o'er;
> Renew it boldly every day,
> And help divine implore.
>
> N'er think the victory won,
> Nor lay thine armour down;
> The work of faith will not be done
> Till thou obtain the crown.

8

Men Under Reconstruction

Orphans are often neglected. So is Nehemiah's seventh memoir. The few who have written on the book spend very little time with the chapter; some ignore it altogether. In doing so, they seem to have forgotten a very important biblical principle, as well as a significant change in the book's direction. A brief word on each is in order.

In his letter to the church at Corinth, the apostle Paul made a point of the fact that every believer is of value and has a specific ministry to the Body. The more prominent members cannot say to the inconspicuous ones, "I have no need of you." Paul declares, "Those members of the body, which seem to be more feeble, are necessary: And those members of the body, which we think to be less honourable, upon these we bestow more abundant honour; and our uncomely parts have more abundant comeliness" (1 Cor 12:22-23).

According to Paul, then, it would appear that this chapter, which to many seems the "more feeble" and unproductive though it is the longest in the whole narrative, is really necessary to the total record. We must pause here and glean what we can that may be profitable for our instruction.

On one matter expositors are quite agreed; that is, with chapter 7 we reach a fork in the road. From the first of these memoirs, we have been concerned chiefly with the *building* of the wall, the purpose that brought Nehemiah back from his life of creature comfort in Persia. But it is clear from the opening verse of chapter 7 that this phase of the work was finished. In a passing remark, Nehemiah refers to the completed project (7:1): *"Now it came to pass, when the wall was built."*

That much of the task was done—a remarkable accomplishment for a band of raw recruits, as we saw in an earlier study. But this did not give Nehemiah reason to relax and fold his hands in admiration of a job well done. Now he must turn his constructive genius to the *builders,* and this equally important task would be at times more demanding and frustrating. Therefore from this chapter onward to the close, we turn from the lifeless stones which were quarried and eventually put in place to make up the wall around the city, to those living stones who put them there. In this light, the memoir is a clear case of men under reconstruction.

We will not begin this study at the beginning, but will purposely bypass the early verses for the moment and read Nehemiah's diary entry in verse 5,

> *And my God put into mine heart to gather together the nobles, and the rulers, and the people, that they might be reckoned by genealogy. And I found a register of the genealogy of them which came up at the first, and found written therein.*

The initial issue which claimed Nehemiah's attention was the *genealogy of the remnant.* There was justification for this. The ancient Jews placed considerable emphasis on their pedigree; their coats of arms were more than bric-a-brac. At least two striking examples appear in the book of Genesis: a formal account of the sons of Jacob near the close of chapter 35, and the exact census of the house of Israel at the time of Jacob's journey into Egypt in chapter 46. Later books record the birth registers of Israel at the time of the wilderness expedition, when king David established the temple service, and in the days of Ezra, Nehemiah's predecessor.

From the natural viewpoint, being able to declare one's pedigree was imperative for an Israelite; uncertainty here would have produced hopeless confusion. Imagine him saying to his friends, "Well, I'm really not quite sure. Sometimes I cherish the hope that I am of the stock of Israel, but at other times I am full of fear that I do not belong at all." Nor would an Israelite hold the equally tenuous view that one could not really be certain he was a true son of Israel until the final day of reckoning. All such ideas, fears, and doubts were foreign to the mind of a true Israelite. He knew he belonged and was prepared to say so.

All of this raises a basic question for *us:* can we declare our pedigree as a Christian? Have we gripped the essential fact and promise of the Christian gospel that "as many as received him, to them gave he power [or the right, or privilege] to become the sons of God, even to them that believe on his name: which were born, not of blood, nor of the will of the flesh, nor of the will of man, but of God" (John 1:12-13)?

Paul could. In one place he avers, "I know whom I have believed, and am persuaded that he is able to keep that which I have committed unto him against that day" (2 Tim 1:12).

Experience in the ministry over many years has convinced me that many cannot say that, would not, or fear to do so. Rather they retreat to those familiar lines,

> Tis a point I long to know;
> Oft it causes anxious thought;
> Do I love my Lord or no;
> Am I His or am I not?
>
> AUTHOR UNKNOWN

Yet this is the believer's *privilege.* One whole epistle in the New Testament was written to confirm that fact. The aged apostle John writes in his first letter, "These things have I written unto you that believe on the name of the Son of God; that ye may know that ye have eternal life" (1 John 5:13). Once that relationship has been secured, we can sing with Lucy A. Bennett,

I am the Lord's! O joy beyond expression,
O sweet response to voice of love Divine;
Faith's joyous "Yes" to the assuring whisper,
"Fear not!" I have redeemed thee; thou art mine.

This privilege of the believer carries with it some oral compulsions. Long ago, the psalmist declared, "Let the redeemed of the LORD say so . . ." (Psalm 107:2). The early apostles of the church took that exhortation seriously, when the council commanded them not to speak or to teach, they replied, "we cannot but speak the things which we have seen and heard," (Acts 4:20). We may conclude that with a compulsion rooted in conviction this faith of ours compels us to speak forth.

However there is another reason for keeping careful birth-registers. Not only did the Jews wish to be able to declare their pedigree, but God Himself wanted known who belonged to the family—and who did not. Observe the diary entry once more at verse 5: *And my God put into mine heart to gather the nobles, and the rulers, and the people, that they might be reckoned by genealogy.*

You see, knowledge of the true seed was essential, especially in the light of the Coming One, our Lord Jesus Christ, who would give an "imperishable glory" to Israel's genealogy. But by the same token, those who could not produce their pedigree would be cut off. This is precisely what we find in Nehemiah's record (7:61-64).

> And these were they which went up also from Tel-melah, Telharesha, Cherub, Addon, and Immer: but they could not shew their father's house, nor their seed, whether they were of Israel. The children of Delaiah, the children of Tobiah, the children of Nekoda, six hundred forty and two. And of the priests: the children of Habaiah, the children of Koz, the children of Barzillai, which took one of the daughters of Barzillai the Gileadite to wife, and was called after their name. These sought their register among those that were reckoned by gene-

alogy, but it was not found: therefore were they, as polluted,
put from the priesthood.

What solemn words, these. Families *in* Israel, but not *of* Israel. And mentioned by name!

In this context God has not left Himself without a witness to
us all. Remember the Savior's searching word: "Many will
say to me in that day, Lord, Lord, have we not prophesied in
thy name? and in thy name have cast out devils? and in thy
name done many wonderful works? And then will I profess
unto them, I never knew you: depart from me, ye that work
iniquity" (Matt 7:22-23).

John's description of these professors is equally stern. He
writes, "They went out from us, but they were not of us; for
if they had been of us, they would no doubt have continued with
us: but they went out, that they might be made manifest that
they were not all of us" (1 John 2:19).

What of the end of all such? "And if anyone's name was not
found written in the book of life, he was thrown into the lake of
fire" (Rev 20:15, NASB).

Once the remnant could prove citizenship, there was work to
do. This brings us to the second major thrust in this long chapter, namely, the *delegation of responsibility.*

Before we look at three main groups cited for their work and
assigned particular tasks, we must say a word about Hanani,
Nehemiah's own brother. He deserves honorable mention. This
man's bringing Nehemiah the grim news about the state of
Jerusalem had resulted in our friend's response to God's call.
Now, with the city newly fortified by the completed wall, and
its temple service fully organized and operating, the city was
ready for someone to guide her community life. This strategic
position was entrusted to Hanani, together with Hananiah, the
ruler of the palace, who feared the Lord above many.

As Jamieson notes, "The piety of Hananiah is especially
mentioned as the ground of his eminent fidelity in the discharge

of all his duties, and consequently, the reason of the confidence which Nehemiah reposed in him, for he was fully persuaded that Hananiah's fear of God would preserve him from those temptations to treachery and unfaithfulness which he was likely to encounter on the governor's departure from Jerusalem."[1]

For all his splended qualifications, Hanani could not do the work alone. To establish order, to promote a proper spirit of worship, and to care for the sacred things of the temple, he needed the help of others. Thus we come to three groups who are singled out from among the people: the *porters,* the *singers,* and the *Levites.* All of them are mentioned by Nehemiah in verse 1. *"Now it came to pass, when the wall was built, and I had set up the doors, and the porters and the singers and the Levites were appointed."*

These same groups are cited again in verses 43-45, where numbers are supplied in addition to the names. Nehemiah considers them important enough to record them as follows:

> *The Levites: the children of Jeshua, of Kadmiel, and of the children of Hodevah, seventy and four. The singers: the children of Asaph, an hundred forty and eight. The porters: the children of Shallum, the children of Ater, the children of Talmon, the children of Akkub, the children of Hatita, the children of Shobai, an hundred thirty and eight.*

They are mentioned once more at the very end of this long chapter, in 7:73: *"So the priests, and the Levites, and the porters, and the singers dwelt . . . in their cities."*

The completed wall served a twofold purpose: it received those who were true Israelites; it refused those who did not belong. I gather, from an earlier reference in the chapter, that the porters were the gatekeepers appointed to secure the gates of the city until the sun was high on the horizon, and then to stand guard. They were watchmen, admitting only those who had a lawful claim to enter the city. In this way they preserved the *purity* of the city and its inhabitants.

Those porters have a patent word for our generation. Often in the church of God there are indefiniteness and compromise in the area of biblical belief and behavior. Spiritual men who will exercise godly discernment are needed to maintain the purity and holy character of the family of God and to welcome those who are true believers and sincere behavers. To use our Lord's own words in John 10:3, to them "the porter openeth." Speaking to the twelve concerning His return and the need to watch and pray, the Saviour said, "It is like a man, away on a journey, who upon leaving his house and putting his slaves in charge, assigning to each one his task, also commanded the doorkeeper to stay on the alert" (Mark 13:34, NASB).

The apostle Paul is even more specific in his admonition to the elders at Ephesus,

> Take heed therefore unto yourselves, and all the flock, over which the Holy Ghost hath made you overseers, to feed the church of God, which he hath purchased with his own blood. For I know this, that after my departing shall grievous wolves enter in among you, not sparing the flock. Also of your own selves shall men arise, speaking perverse things, to draw away disciples after them. Therefore watch (Acts 20:28-31).

The *singers* are mentioned next. Verse 44 speaks of the children of Asaph, 148, who made up the sanctuary choir. Those familiar with the long sweep of the Old Testament will recall some earlier instances when singers were called upon to provide inspiration. Following the dramatic crossing of the Red Sea, Moses led the people in singing a song of triumph. Following Israel's victory over Jabin, king of Canaan, Deborah and Barak performed a duet. David and his son Solomon after him both made considerable use of choirs on festive occasions "to make one sound to be heard in praising and thanking the LORD" (2 Chron 5:13).

On the occasion of Dallas Seminary's fiftieth anniversary, an appropriate hymnal was prepared. In the prologue to *Hymns of Jubilee,* Dr. Edwin C. Deibler of the seminary faculty wrote,

> From earliest times, the people of God have employed music to give expression of their adoration of the triune God. The Old Testament, which provided the original Scriptures of the church, is replete with psalms and hymns of praise to Jehovah. The New Testament incorporates phrases which seem by their form to indicate that they were first used by assemblies of believers to express their understanding of Christian truth and their love for the Saviour. Succeeding generations of Christians—to our present day—have adapted poetry set to music to pour their adoration, praise, aspirations and prayers. Often, perhaps nearly always, such expressions have exceeded in intensity the actual life-styles of the congregations who employed them. The editors of *Victorious Life Hymns* have aptly noted this truth: "If Christian experience were, even for a period of one week, brought to the level of Christian hymns, a great revival would sweep over the world."[2]

For many years now, it has been a personal conviction that the spirit of praise expressed in appropriate music is the spirit of power. Such music is not incidental; it is *important.* It is not preliminary; it is *preparatory.* Moreover, it is not sentimental; it is *scriptural.*

No wonder Nehemiah had a choir.

Believing that "every good hymn learned and loved is another window through which the worshipping soul looks toward heaven," let us emulate him.

Finally, we come to the *Levites.* According to the memoir, there were seventy-four of them. In order to appreciate their function here, we must go back to the book of Numbers and read Moses' directions concerning them.

> But thou shalt appoint the Levites over the tabernacle of testimony, and over all the vessels thereof, and over all things that belong to it: they shall bear the tabernacle, and all the vessels

thereof; and they shall minister unto it, and shall encamp round about the tabernacle. And when the tabernacle setteth forward, the Levites shall take it down: and when the tabernacle is to be pitched, the Levites shall set it up . . . , the Levites shall keep the charge of the tabernacle of testimony (Num 1:50-53).

First Chronicles 6:48, confirming that this was done in later times, says, "The Levites were appointed unto all manner of service of the tabernacle of the house of God."

In a word, what was the chief task of the Levites? The repetition of one word in the texts just cited compels us to say their task was the "tabernacle." To borrow an expression from Paul's testimony, the Levites could say, "For us to live is the tabernacle." Living for the tabernacle, the Levites were consumed with all its care.

We recognize that the tabernacle symbolizes our Lord Jesus Christ. And in this sense, those Levites were the protectors of the *person* of Him who watched over the city in which He had been pleased to set His name.

As we reflect upon these three groups which Nehemiah singled out from a company of some 42,360 (not counting others who served in menial tasks), three words stand forth with respect to the threefold task of every company of believers: the *porters* preserved the *purity* of the city of God. So must we. The *singers* provided the *praise* in the city of God. So should we. And the *Levites* protected the *Person* of the city of God. And so may we!

9

The Master Blueprint

The eighth memoir brings us to a significant point in our study of this interesting book. In chapter 6, the wall was completed. In chapter 7, the genealogy of the city dwellers was examined, and provision made for the security of the city. Now we are ready for the establishment of the authority of the Word of God. The order here is instructive. While the wall may have been built, and the Israelites duly gathered and organized, only the Word of God and obedience to it could keep the people in their new experience.

Apropos the subject before us is this nugget gleaned from many sources across the years: The Bible is the total source of all that we are to preach and teach. We do not *create* the message, we only *communicate* it. And in doing so we prepare the hearts of the people of God for the Spirit's work and blessing.

To a remarkable degree, these words summarize the eighth memoir.

We begin with *the setting* for the chapter. In the opening verse Nehemiah tells us, *"And all the people gathered themselves together as one man into the street that was before the water gate."*

What an imposing spectacle! But is it not always so when a great congregation gathers in solemn assembly? Especially was this congregation imposing, for the people were ripe for a fresh invasion of divine blessing. And mark this: they were *all* there. Moreover, they were all *there*. These have always been precur-

sors to a visitation from God. Vance Havner makes a very
practical application of this in his study dealing with Elijah the
Tishbite. "I do not believe," writes Havner, "that the ravens
would have fed Elijah anywhere else, nor would the widow
woman have appeared anywhere else except 'THERE.' God
did not say, 'Elijah, ramble around as you please and I will
provide for you.' 'THERE' was the place of God's will for
Elijah—the place of His Purpose, the place of His Power and
the place of His Provision."[1] A bit later, the author concludes,
"He is responsible for our upkeep when we follow His directions, but He is not responsible for any expenses not included
in His schedule."[2]

I like that, not only because it was true of Elijah, but because the principle is true for all time. The question is always
relevant: are you *there?* Thomas was not there that first evening
of our Lord's resurrection, and he missed seeing the Saviour.
The band of believers was there on the day of Pentecost and
received the outpouring of the Holy Spirit. So it was with Nehemiah and the remnant; they were there.

In this case, where was *there?* Before the Water Gate. You
will recall that in our study of chapter three, we referred to the
gates of the city and suggested their spiritual significance for
the child of God. The Water Gate was, in our judgment, a picture of the Word of God. If this be so, how interesting it is
that on this high and holy occasion of Nehemiah's "Back to the
Bible Hour," we find the people gathered by *that* gate. I do not
think it was coincidental.

Then it happened: The cry went up for Ezra the scribe to
*"bring the book of the law of Moses, which the Lord had com-
manded to Israel."* The setting of this chapter gives way now
to *the scroll.*

It is a subject of conjecture as to where Ezra had been before this hour. He is not mentioned by Nehemiah as being
among those who shared in the rebuilding of the wall. Nor was
he involved in the internal problem of the oppression of the

poor. Is it possible that he had returned to Babylon? Or that
his attempts at religious reforms had been frustrated, and he
sought retirement from active ministry? We do not know. This
much we do know: When the cry went up from that multitude,
"Bring the book!", Ezra was *there* with the sacred scroll, possibly the only copy of the Law available at that time.

And what did our friend Nehemiah do in this situation? It
must be said to his everlasting credit that when Ezra emerged
on the scene in response to the people, this savior of Israel
modestly retired into the background.

> A finer proof of the unselfish humility of the young statesman
> cannot be imagined. Though at the height of his power, hav-
> ing frustrated the many evil designs of his enemies and com-
> pleted his stupendous task of fortifying the city of his fathers
> in spite of the most vexatious difficulties, the successful patriot
> is not in the least degree flushed with victory. In the quietest
> manner possible he steps aside and yields the first place to the
> recluse, the student, the writer, the teacher.[3]

What a fine display in flesh and blood of what the New Testament would later urge: "in honour preferring one another"
(Rom 12:10).

To return to Ezra, now that he occupied the attention of the
congregation, mark the manner in which he met this welcomed
request; it is unique in biblical history. Here we see the priest-
scribe, the precious scroll in his hand, standing on a temporary
wooden platform so that he might be visible to the people. With
Levites supporting him on either side, he read the Law before
the gathered assembly.

Hitherto, the Law had been a matter of private study among
a select few. And for obvious reason: the Scriptures were simply not available for public consumption. Consequently, religious assemblies for the masses were almost unknown. Now,
all that was changed; the sacred writings were public domain—
not only for adults but for children also ("those that could un-

derstand"). This had been the divine intention from the early
days of Israel under Moses. Again and again, the Lord had
given instructions regarding the teaching of His precepts to the
family, "that your days may be multiplied, and the days of your
children (Deut 11:21).

The fact of the divine intention is evidenced further in the
life of the young church, especially in her first five centuries.
The Word of God was the indispensable source and sustainer of
life for the people of God. Paul wrote to Timothy, "From a
child thou hast known the holy scriptures" (2 Tim 3:15). He
urged the Christians at Colosse, "Let the word of Christ dwell
in you richly in all wisdom; teaching and admonishing one another in psalms and hymns and spiritual songs" (Col 3:16). We
must add the witness of the church Fathers. Said Cyprian, the
illustrious bishop of Carthage, to his African flock, "Let the
Scriptures be in your hands." Wrote Jerome to the widow De-
metrias, "I cannot sufficiently urge you to devote yourself to the
reading of the Bible." Some of the poorer believers copied out
parts of the Bible for themselves.

From these brief glimpses, it should be apparent that the
Bible was not the church's book; it was regarded as every Christian's book—to be held, to be read, and obeyed.

My personal experience with the professing church in our
times leads me to say that, while there are many churches where
the Word of God is opened and taught, the greater part of those
who frequent the house of God are turned away with little to
eat. As a result, ignorance and indifference abound. This
ought not to be. Ezra and the remnant of Israel and the early
church are viable challenges to us all to be faithful keepers of
the springs of Scripture.

What was the indirect result of the ministry of Ezra and his
associates? Nehemiah tells us (8:8): *"So they read in the book
in the law of God distinctly, and gave the sense, and caused
them to understand the reading."*

It has been suggested that this may well have been the first time in Judah that the Scriptures were explained and made the basis for faith. If this be so, at long last, it was not the priest who led the people, but the "scribe of the words of the commandments of the Lord, and of His statutes to Israel" who shared the sacred scroll. Henceforth instruction was to be the ground for the people's faith. This expounding of the Scriptures would be a precursor of the Christian expository sermon as we know it today. Surely the example of Ezra on this occasion should challenge every servant of Christ to minister the truth of God in such a way as to cause the people to understand, or as the Quakers were wont to say, "to speak to the condition of their hearts."

We have considered the setting of the memoir and the exposition of the scroll. We come now to *the results* which attended the ministry of the Word. The text suggests four.

In the first place, the communication of the message resulted in *worship*. Several selections from Nehemiah's memoir make this clear. Note the following: verse 3, *"and the ears of all the people were attentive unto the book of the law,"* verse 5, *"And when he opened it, all the people stood up."* And when Ezra had read the book and blessed the people, they answered (8:6): *"Amen, Amen, with lifting up their hands: and they bowed their heads, and worshipped the Lord with their faces to the ground."*

What a delightful response to the Word of God! They worshiped. I fear Tozer spoke to our condition when he wrote,

> We have lost our spirit of worship and our ability to withdraw inwardly to meet God in adoring silence. Modern Christianity is simply not producing the kind of Christian who can appreciate or experience the life in the Spirit. The words, "Be still, and know that I am God," mean next to nothing to the self-confident, bustling worshiper in this middle of the twentieth century.[4]

On the other hand, as we dare to come near the holy men and women of the past, we cannot escape the heat of their de-

sire after God. This was so in Scripture; it was equally so in
the later history of the church. Who of us could ever improve
on those lines from Bernard of Clairvaux as that modest monk
gave expression to his deepest worship experience?

> We taste Thee, O Thou Living Bread,
> And long to feast upon Thee still:
> We drink of Thee, the Fountainhead,
> And thirst our souls from Thee to fill.

That is worship. The Word did it.

Second, the reading of the Word resulted in *weeping*. At the
end of verse 9, Nehemiah records, *"All the people wept, when
they heard the words of the law."*

This evidence of grief was not because the people rejected
the precepts of the Law, but rather because they recognized
their miserable imperfections in the light of that Law. In that
light they suddenly discovered that the robe of righteousness in
which they had been standing so proudly was in fact a wretched
garment.

The Bible has a way of doing just that. The Word of God
gives the cutting edge not only to the gospel which saves men in
the first place, but to the truth which edifies the believer. Inspired by the Holy Spirit, the Bible is like a fire, like a hammer, like a sword, like a mirror. But the important issue is
this: what is our response to it? Do we sit in judgment on that
Word? Or do we let that Word sit in judgment on us? A world
of difference lies between these. Luke, in his gospel, puts the
issue in bold relief when he cites two reactions to our Lord's
words. The Pharisees and the lawyers listened, but they "rejected the counsel of God against themselves." The people and
the publicans, when they heard His words, "justified God"
(Luke 7:29-30).

Thus it happened to the Jewish remnant. Under the lashes
of the Law, they let the Word of God sit in judgment on them,
and they were moved to tears of conviction and confession.

They did not need Solomon to tell them that there is a time to weep.

The reading of that Law did something else. Having led them to worship and weeping, it now called them to action. In all probability it was Ezra, supported by Nehemiah and the Levites, who gave the command (8:10).

> *Then he said unto them, Go your way, eat the fat, and drink the sweet, and send portions unto them for whom nothing is prepared: for this day is holy unto our Lord: neither be ye sorry; for the joy of the Lord is your strength. . . . And all the people went their way to eat, and to drink, and to send portions, and to make great mirth, because they had understood the words that were declared unto them.*

Ezra and Nehemiah understood that now that the Law had done its inward work, the thoughts of the people should be directed toward those without for whom nothing had been prepared. In a practical display of true missions, they were to go and to share. Borrowing the words of the four leprous men in the days of Elisha, the leaders were saying in effect, "You do not well; this day is a day of good tidings, and you hold your peace. Now therefore, go" (cf. 2 Kings 7:9).

And so they *went!*

We must not pass over that remarkable expression which has endeared itself to believers down through the years: *"The joy of the Lord is your strength"* (8:10). Rejoicing in the Lord is one of the great divine ideas of Scripture. Never was that more true than at this very hour in Israel's history. Their fathers, some forty thousand of them, had been delivered from Babylon. To be sure, things had not been easy. But the Temple was rebuilt and its services restored. Now, after some seventy years, the city wall was in place and the enemies defeated. Surely this was a time for joy.

Need we trace the parallel? Have we not been redeemed by the precious blood of Christ? Have we not been brought out of terrible captivity? For these and a thousand more blessings shall we not rejoice in the Lord?

How appropriate then to say with Habakkuk, "I will joy in the God of my salvation" (Hab 3:18).

All the people worshiped. They wept. They went. And now they *wrought.* Nehemiah here details the incident (8:13-17).

> *And on the second day were gathered together the chief of the fathers of all the people, the priests, and the Levites, unto Ezra the scribe, even to understand the words of the law. And they found written in the law which the Lord had commanded by Moses, that the children of Israel should dwell in booths in the feast of the seventh month: and that they should publish and proclaim in all their cities, and in Jerusalem, saying, Go forth unto the mount, and fetch olive branches, and pine branches . . . and branches of thick trees, to make booths, as it is written. So the people went forth, and brought them, and made themselves booths, every one upon the roof of his house, and in their courts, and in the courts of the house of God, and in the street of the water gate, and in the street of the gate of Ephraim. And all the congregation of them that were come again out of the captivity made booths: and sat under the booths: for since the days of Jeshua the son of Nun unto that day had not the children of Israel done so.*

Here is an amazing thing. Such an observance as cited by Nehemiah had not been seen in Israel in a thousand years. Even the days of David in all his glory, and those of Solomon his son, had not witnessed anything like it. How was it then that it happened here? The answer is plain: they heard the Law of the Lord and obeyed it.

Perhaps the very word they heard that day the Law was read was Jehovah's instruction to His people regarding the feast of the seventh month. He had said, "Ye shall dwell in booths seven days; all that are Israelites born shall dwell in booths: that your generations may know that I made the children of Israel to dwell in booths, when I brought them out of the land of Egypt: I am the LORD your God" (Lev 23:42-43).

So attuned was the remnant to the Word of God that when they discovered that God had commanded booths, they built booths. It was that simple.

And with what result? Nehemiah adds an important postscript: *"And there was very great gladness."*

Of course. As Harry Allan Ironside suggests in part, every true, abiding work of God whether it be the harvesting of souls or the awakening of believers, has been based on "the revealed Word of the Lord." Where you find God's people seeking to know God's Word, you find blessing.

It was so in Josiah's day.

It was so in Hezekiah's day.

It was so in Nehemiah's day.

It may be so in our day!

10

Chips of History

"After the carnival—Lent." Thus Walter F. Adeney, English scholar, begins his perceptive commentary on chapter 9. Only the day before, Ezra and Nehemiah, together with the Levites, had encouraged the people to rejoice and had reminded them that the joy of the Lord was their strength. As a result, the previous memoir ended on a note of thanksgiving. *"There was very great gladness"* is Nehemiah's summary of what happened.

But now all that was changing.

The feast of thanksgiving had lasted for seven days. The day following, set aside for meditation, was a harbinger of what was to take place shortly. Then it happened. On the twenty-fourth day, the people turned from feasting to fasting. They laid aside their festive attire and covered themselves with sackcloth and earth, symbols of humiliation. It seems clear that the Word which they had heard earlier had given them light on their true condition, and now they were ready to give outward expression of that inward work.

Nehemiah records the event in verse 2: *"And the seed of Israel separated themselves from all strangers, and stood and confessed their sins, and the iniquities of their fathers."*

The *attitude* of the people is the first important matter in this chapter. Observe who these people are. Nehemiah speaks of them as the *"seed of Israel."* This nation, unlike any other on

earth, had its roots in God and had been redeemed to Him on
the ground of the Passover lamb. As such, they were not only
the "seed" (9:12) but the "holy seed" (Ezra 9:2), and as such
were to emulate the character of Him who had called them to be
His special people. That this was so can be demonstrated from
many passages of Scripture, but none is more explicit than Ex-
odus 19:4-6. Addressing Himself to Israel through His servant
Moses, God says,

> Ye have seen what I did unto the Egyptians, and how I bare
> you on eagles' wings, and brought you unto myself. Now
> therefore, if ye will obey my voice indeed, and keep my cove-
> nant, then ye shall be a peculiar treasure unto me above all
> people: for all the earth is mine: and ye shall be unto me a
> kingdom of priests, and an holy nation.

Alas, it had not been so. The Jews of the remnant, like their
fathers before them, had allowed their distinct position among
the family of nations to fall into neglect. As a result, they had
mingled with strangers, thereby jeopardizing their identity as
well as their mission in the earth.

Now, through the reading and explanation of the inspired
blueprint, the Scriptures, this failure had come home to their
hearts, and they were prepared to take a first step toward setting
matters right. Their *attitude* found expression initially in separating themselves from all strangers. This was not a case of es-
teeming themselves better than their Gentile neighbors. Nor
were they seeking to attach blame to their Gentile neighbors for
what had happened. The guilt was theirs, and they were saying
so in this present circumstance.

Sequential to separating themselves from strangers, the people *"stood and confessed their sins, and the iniquities of their
fathers."* This is ever God's order. Shown by the word of God
that they had sinned in their associations with strangers, the
people acted upon what they saw and confessed their guilt before the Lord. To confess sin while cleaving to it is mockery.

None of that was here. So determined were they to lay the axe to the root of the tree, that they rehearsed before God not only their own sins, but those of their fathers as well. This was no superficial work of the flesh; it was a deep exposure of their sin for which they had suffered chastisement.

How this atittude must have delighted the heart of God. Through the prophet Isaiah, He had said, "To this man will I look, even to him that is poor and of a contrite spirit, and trembleth at my word" (Isa 66:2). Seven centuries later, the apostle Paul wrote to the Corinthian church, "For if we would judge ourselves, we should not be judged" (1 Cor 11:31). This is the divine pattern. Alan Redpath is right when he observes, "God will never plant the seed of His life upon the soil of a hard, unbroken spirit. He will only plant that seed where the conviction of His Spirit has brought brokenness, where the soil has been watered with the tears of repentance."[1]

In the light of the attitude of Israel, and the appeal of the Word of God to us all, we might be greatly helped in this matter of self-judgment if we shared the prayer of Bessie Porter Head:

> A Breath of Life, come sweeping through us,
> Revive Thy Church, with life and power;
> O Breath of Life, come, cleanse, renew us,
> And fit Thy Church to meet this hour.

> O Wind of God, come bend us, break us,
> Till humbly we confess our need;
> Then in Thy tenderness remake us,
> Revive, restore, for this we plead.

We come now to the second major section of the memoir (9:4-37), which concerns the prayer of the Levites on behalf of the people. Our interest in that prayer—incidentally the longest in Scripture—has to do with its *arrangement*. Reading it reminds one of a number of the historical psalms, such as Psalm 74, 78, 89, 105 and 106. They give a variegated picture of Israel's past, and show how God revealed Himself through great historical landmarks. I call them "chips of history."

As we look more closely at the arrangement of the prayer, we can distinguish two major chords: the *faithfulness* of God, and the *failure* of man. It has been rightly observed:

> The method of the prayer is to bring these chords into view alternately, as they are illustrated in the History of Israel. The result is like a drama of several acts, and three scenes in each act. Although we see progress and a continuous heightening of effect, there is a startling resemblance between the successive acts, and the relative characters of the scenes remain the same throughout.[2]

Inasmuch as the several acts and their corresponding scenes are repetitious, we will confine ourselves to just one act and to just one of the corresponding threefold scenes. Hopefully, in doing so, we shall be able to give the true flow of the whole.

The first act is the obvious choice because it not only embraces the pattern of the whole, but it begins with a most important basis for intercession. Nehemiah makes a point of this at the end of verse 4, where he records that the Levites *"cried with a loud voice unto their God."*

Immediately thereafter, a second company of choristers called upon the assembled congregation in the temple courts to rise and join in the adoration (9:5-6).

> *Stand up and bless the Lord your God for ever and ever: and blessed be thy glorious name, which is exalted above all blessing and praise. Thou, even thou, art Lord alone; thou hast made heaven, the heaven of heavens with all their host, the earth, and all things that are therein, the seas, and all that is therein, and thou preservest them all, and the host of heaven worshippeth thee.*

Do not miss it. The prayer opens with an outburst of praise to the Author and Finisher of all things. This is more than a

cold invocation of Jewish monotheism; it is the practical confession of the supremacy of God in His world which He not only
made, but sustains. From highest to lowest, He is adored.

Again, it is right and fitting that we approach our blessed God
in an attitude of pure worship. Not only is this ideal prepara-
tion for our petitions which follow, but it enables us to see
things in their proper order. "He who has once seen God," one
has written, "knows how to look at the world and his own
heart."[3] It is true that we can best trace the course of the val-
leys from the mountain top.

But now let us follow our friends, the Levites, as they particu-
larize their prayer and count their blessings one by one. Nehemiah listens and records some of God's ways (9:7-15).

> *Thou . . . didst choose Abram, and broughtest him forth out
> of Ur of the Chaldees, and gavest him the name of Abra-
> ham . . . and madest a covenant with him . . . and didst see the
> affliction of our fathers in Egypt, and heardest their cry by the
> Red sea; and shewedst signs and wonders upon Pharaoh. . . .
> And thou didst divide the sea before them . . . and their perse-
> cutors thou threwest into the deeps. . . . Moreover thou leddest
> them in the day by a cloudy pillar; and in the night by a pillar
> of fire. . . . and spakest with them from heaven . . . and madest
> known unto them thy holy sabbath . . . and broughtest forth
> water for them out of the rock . . . and promisedst them that
> they should go in to possess the land. . . .*

What a review of the free and generous favor of a faithful
God to His people, and that without any merit on their part; all
was God's doing. He chose. He gave. He made. He saw. He
heard. He spoke. He promised.

The second scene reveals another chip of history. That a
change of scenes is in prospect becomes evident by the inser-
tion of that conjunction "But" at the beginning of verse 16. Integrity compelled Nehemiah to put down just what he heard
(9:16-18).

> *But they and our fathers dealt proudly, and hardened their necks, and hearkened not to thy commandments, and refused to obey, neither were mindful of thy wonders that thou didst among them; but hardened their necks, and in their rebellion appointed a captain to return to their bondage: but thou art a God ready to pardon, gracious and merciful, slow to anger, and of great kindness, and forsookest them not. Yea, when they had made them a molten calf, and said, This is thy God that brought thee up out of Egypt, and had wrought great provocations.*

What an ugly picture of Israel's ingratitude and ultimate rebellion.

Then comes the marvelous third scene (9:19-20).

> *Yet thou in thy manifold mercies forsookest them not in the wilderness: the pillar of the cloud departed not from them by day, to lead them in the way; neither the pillar of fire by night, to shew them light, and the way wherein they should go. Thou gavest also thy good spirit to instruct them, and withheldest not thy manna from their mouth, and gavest them water for their thirst.*

That should have been enough to melt the hardest heart. The mercies of God are enumerated: the cloud by day, the fire by night, the manna for food, the water for their thirst, and over all, His "good spirit" to instruct them in the way. Thus it was that He not only displayed His great forbearance in the presence of ingratitude and rebellion but gave fresh tokens of His grace where sin did abound.

As we think on that first great act with its scenes of divine faithfulness, human failure, and divine deliverance, what can we take for ourselves? What could the Holy Spirit be saying to us in all these things? If Israel, who received such unmistakable tokens of God's choosing, concern, care, and consideration was unresponsive to the point of ingratitude and rebellion, where is hope for us? From our side, there is none. Apart from divine

invasion, man, whoever he is, is a ruined instrument by nature.
There are no blue ribbons in our pedigree; we all come from
bad stock. The Bible says so.

For confirmation, read again the first three chapters of Paul's
letter to the church at Rome. When he finishes with the human race, the race is finished! He has every mouth stopped—
that of Jew and Gentile alike—and the whole world declared
guilty before God. But note, man's guilt is put on display so
that the grace of God in Jesus Christ might be equally displayed
to all who will receive Him by faith. This gives the widest possible scope for that word in Romans 4:5, "But to him that
worketh not, but believeth on him that justifieth the ungodly,
his faith is counted for righteousness."

When we have come to that place, we are ready to sing with
Zinzendorf,

> Jesus, Thy blood and righteousness
> My beauty are, my glorious dress;
> 'Midst flaming worlds, in these arrayed,
> With joy shall I lift up my head.[4]

Further detailing Israel's history, the prayer moves to a conclusion at verse 37. We have considered the *attitude* of the people and the *arrangement* of their prayer. It remains now to say
a word about the *affirmation* of their purpose. Note Nehemiah's
statement in the closing verse of chapter 9, and then glance at
the long list of signatories catalogued in chapter 10. *"And because of all this we make a sure covenant, and write it; and our
princes, Levites, and priests, seal unto it."*

Nehemiah is undoubtedly remembering the long review just
covered and its alternating revelations of God's faithfulness and
man's failure.

What did they sign? A *"sure covenant,"* replies Nehemiah.
And what were its contents? Chiefly, three articles.

First of all, they faced up to the Law's demands affecting
their *domestic* relationships. At the time of the original entry

into Canaan, God had set out strict provisions regarding marriage with the pagan nations among whom they dwelt. Regarding this critical matter, the Law of God read as follows:

> When the LORD thy God shall bring thee into the land whither thou goest to possess it, and hath cast out many nations before thee . . . and when the LORD thy God shall deliver them before thee; thou shalt smite them, and utterly destroy them; thou shalt make no covenant with them, nor shew mercy unto them: neither shalt thou make marriages with them; thy daughter thou shalt not give unto his son, nor his daughter shalt thou take unto thy son. For they will turn away thy son from following me, that they may serve other gods: so will the anger of the LORD be kindled against you, and destroy thee suddenly (Deut 7:1-4).

At this point in time the Jews knew only too well that they had disobeyed that command, and it was imperative that they do something about it. They agreed, as Nehemiah records in his diary entry for that day: *"That we would not give our daughters unto the people of the land, nor take their daughters for our sons"* (10:30).

A second mark of Jewish distinctiveness was the observance of the Sabbath. Again the Law was clear on the matter. God had instructed His people through Moses,

> Remember the sabbath day, to keep it holy. Six days shalt thou labour, and do all thy work: But the seventh day is a sabbath of the LORD thy God: in it thou shalt not do any work, nor thy son, nor thy daughter, thy manservant, nor thy maidservant, nor thy cattle, nor thy stranger that is within thy gates: for in six days the LORD made heaven and earth, the sea, and all that in them is, and rested the seventh day: wherefore the LORD blessed the sabbath day, and hallowed it (Exod 20:8-11).

As they read that text, they reacted positively to it. Nehemiah notes that they bound themselves to the Law that *"they would not buy on the sabbath day"* (10:31). Trading with their Gentile neighbors, while legitimate on most days, was forbidden on the Sabbath. That law affected their *commercial* relationships.

Finally, we must not overlook the loving concern which the people had for the house of God and those who ministered there. The expression *"his house"* appears nine times in the memoir and seems to concentrate on two things. One is devotion to *giving* (10:32): *"We made ordinances for us, to charge ourselves yearly with the third part of a shekel for the service of the house of our God."* The second is devotion to *worship* in God's house (10:39): *"And we will not forsake the house of our God."*

Here again, the Law was explicit. The Lord spoke to Moses, saying,

> When thou takest the sum of the children of Israel after their number, then shall they give every man a ransom for his soul unto the LORD, when thou numberest them; that there be no plague among them, when thou numberest them. This they shall give, every one that passeth among them that are numbered, half a shekel, after the shekel of the sanctuary . . . an half shekel shall be the offering of the LORD. . . . The rich shall not give more, and the poor shall not give less than half a shekel, when they give an offering unto the LORD, to make an atonement for your souls. And thou shalt take the atonement money of the children of Israel, and shall appoint it for the service of the tabernacle of the congregation; that it may be a memorial unto the children of Israel before the LORD, to make an atonement for your souls (Exod 30:12-16).

Now they did as God had commanded them, and in so doing they committed themselves to the Law affecting their *spiritual* relationships.

What a grand alliance had been compacted! These laws to which God's people gave their assent covered domestic, commercial, and spiritual obligations. What incentive for us to walk in the steps of the Saviour, not now impelled by *law,* but inspired by *love*—love for Him because of all that He has done for us! Surely we are to emulate the disciplined, humbled people of Israel who, having seen the error of their ways, committed themselves to walk in the Law of the Lord.

Be it ours to say with the psalmist, "Order my steps in thy word."

11

Dedicating the City of God

Two words provide the key to this historic moment which Nehemiah now records: *postponement* and *commencement*.

It is a curious feature of this restoration of Israel that in each of the three expeditions there was deliberate delay. When Zerubbabel and Jeshua led that first expedition for the express purpose of building the *Temple,* the work began in the days of Cyrus, but was not completed until the reign of Darius. Ezra, in all probability having the Law of God in his possession, led back the second contingent for the explicit purpose of establishing the *worship* of Jehovah under the pedagogy of that Law. Yet he did not find a suitable opportunity to proclaim that Law until some years later. With our friend Nehemiah, the pattern prevailed. The wall had been finished with amazing celerity—in fifty-two days—yet there it stood, stones and mortar, awaiting attention to other matters.[1]

Perhaps we are better able now to explain the postponement of the dedication; it was not without purpose. To quote Adeney, "May we not say that in every similar case the personal consecration must precede the material? The city is what its citizens make it."[2] Until now, despite the completion of the wall, the city of Jerusalem was little more than a "lodge in a garden of cucumbers." What the city needed was *people*—people who would reside there and accept the responsibilities of citizenship. Such a need was not easily met. While the wall was finished, houses within that wall were not the best, so that life would be rigorous and demanding. It is no surprise, then, to pick up the thread of Nehemiah's diary and find this record (11:2): *"And the people blessed all the men, that willingly offered themselves to dwell at Jerusalem."*

One-tenth of the total number of the remnant, all willing ones, took up residence in the city surrounded by its wonderful wall. The names of many of these urban dwellers are cataloged. Verse 3 of chapter 11 through verse 26 of chapter 12 stands as the first city directory issued by the city council of Jerusalem. Thus the postponement fulfilled its purpose.

We come now to the second key word: commencement. Scholars who are familiar with the Hebrew language maintain that in our English version of the Bible the word *"dedicate"* is made to stand for two totally distinct Hebrew terms. The one, the more spiritual in tone, means to *consecrate* or *to make holy.* It is employed where priestly sacrifices are involved. The other word means to *initiate,* that is, to mark the beginning of something. It is the more secular term, and is the term used by Nehemiah in his memoir. It signalizes a commencement, a new beginning. In this regard, *"dedicate"* is but another display of the divine heritage of the new—a new covenant, a new heart, and eventually a new heaven and a new earth.[3]

The dedication was inspiring indeed, particularly for Nehemiah. It was the occasion when all his aspirations, born so long ago in far-off Persia, were brought to a grand consummation. It was his finest hour. But it was not his alone; Nehemiah was mindful of his beloved people who shared his vision and enthusiasm. Thus his narrative notes the people who came from the villages and plains around the city to observe the occasion with instruments and choirs.

How did the commencement program begin? First was the act of *purification.* Nehemiah tells us (12:30), *"And the priests and the Levites purified themselves, and purified the people, and the gates, and the wall."*

The fresh, clean beginning called for a fresh cleansing. The principle of purity and exhortation to purity are woven securely into the fabric of Scripture. The whole Levitical system was built upon the divine directive, "I am the LORD your God: ye shall therefore sanctify yourselves, and ye shall be holy; for I am holy" (Lev 11:44). David asks the question, "Who may ascend into the hill of the LORD? or who shall stand in his holy place? He that hath clean hands, and a pure heart" (Psalm 24:3-4).

Just what means of purification were used at this time is not stated in the text. During the days of the wilderness wanderings, the priests washed in water before fulfilling their services (Exod 30:17-21). And in the ashes of the red heifer, provision was made for all manner of defilement of priests and people (Num 19). We can only conjecture that the same procedure was followed as that employed by Hezekiah on the occasion of his national purification (2 Chron 29:17-24).

Observe where the cleanup campaign began. It started with the priests and the Levites. This is as it should be, for the Word of God is clear: they who bear the vessels of the Lord must be clean. Or as the ancient rabbis were wont to say, "First be trimmed thyself, and then adorn thy brethren." But having begun there, the priests purified the people, the gates, and the wall.

The purification ceremony is a challenging example to the church of God. Oh, that we might be heard to pray, "Lord, make us clean in our house!"

Next to be observed on that great day was a *procession*. From the description of Nehemiah in his diary it is evident that this was an organized affair. Included were the representative classes of his people—priests, princes, and Levites. These formed two great companies. Ezra, the priest, accompanied by singers and trumpeters, set out toward the right, going south. In like manner Nehemiah set out, going left and north, and likewise accompanied by musicians. At the end of the procession, the two companies met at the eastern side of the city op-

posite the Mount of Olives and close to the Temple area. There
they broke into an enthusiastic burst of praise.[4]

Who conceived this procession? And what purpose did it
serve? I think Nehemiah makes clear that he was responsible
for the parade, and that he intended it should serve a proper
and important purpose. After all, Nehemiah could never forget
the unselfish labors of his people as they worked privately, each
on his own part of the wall. Now that the task was finished, it
seemed right that the people should march publicly, not to
glorify the processionists, but as a public witness to their unity.
If Sabrine Baring-Gould had lived in those thrilling days, we
might have heard the procession singing,

> Like a mighty army moves the Church of God;
> Brothers, we are treading where the saints have trod.
> We are not divided, all one body we—
> One in hope and doctrine, one in charity.

While they did not have the song, they did have the spirit of
it.

The New Testament affirms the rectitude of what Nehemiah
did. In his letter to the Ephesian church concerning the gifts
entrusted to individual believers, Paul makes the point that gifts
and their corresponding functions are not to be exercised in a
corner, but rather for the good of the whole body. As he says,
"From whom the whole body fitly joined together and compacted by that which every joint supplieth, according to the
effectual working in the measure of every part, maketh increase
of the body unto the edifying of itself in love" (Eph 4:16).

I believe that had Nehemiah known that text, he would have
responded, "That's why I did it!"

Over the years now, I have had hanging in my study a lovely,
practical reminder of this truth. It bears the simple title "The
Carpenter's Tools." Brother Hammer, because he was too
noisy, was asked by the other tools to leave the shop. But he
said, "If I am to leave this carpenter's shop, Brother Gimlet

must go too. He is so insignificant that he makes very little impression." Brother Gimlet arose and said, "All right, but Brother Screw must also go. You have to turn him around again and again to get him anywhere." Brother Screw responded, "If you wish, I will go, but Brother Plane must leave also. All his work is on the surface; there is no depth to it." Brother Plane replied, "Well, Brother Rule will have to withdraw if I do, for he is always measuring folks as though he were the only one who is right." Brother Rule complained against Brother Sandpaper, saying, "I just don't care; he is rougher than he ought to be. He is always rubbing people the wrong way."

In the midst of the discussion, the Carpenter of Nazareth walked in to perform His day's work. He put on His apron and went to the bench to make a pulpit from which to preach the gospel to the poor. He employed the screw, the gimlet, the sandpaper, the saw, the hammer, the plane, and all the other tools.

After the day's work was over, and the pulpit was finished, Brother Saw arose and said, "Brethren, I perceive that all of us are laborers together with God."

And so we are.

At verse 42, Nehemiah records a third important aspect of that day of dedication,

> *Also that day they offered great sacrifices, and rejoiced: for God had made them rejoice with great joy: the wives also and the children rejoiced: so that the joy of Jerusalem was heard even afar off.*

Was there a cause? Indeed there was. What changes had taken place since that dark, lonely night when Nehemiah made his circuit of the ruined city, its gates burned and its people in reproach. All that was changed now; the leader and his loyal colleagues had every right to be glad. As has been observed, "The Thanksgiving would arise out of a grateful acknowledgement of the goodness of God in leading the work of building the walls through many perils and disappointments to its present consummation."[5]

Perhaps more than at any other time, the people really understood Nehemiah's great secret for them. They found their strength in the joy of the Lord—a joy in which the women and children present on occasions of national festivities—would gladly share. So the joy of Jerusalem was heard afar off.[6]

As we reflect on the spirit in the young church during the apostolic period, few things were more characteristic of the believers than their exuberant joy. This abiding effect of the "good tidings" was undoubtedly one of the leading factors in the rapid spread of the gospel. Those who witness such joy in people whose lives have known only frustration and trouble are likely to believe that such people possess something worth having.

This is a word in season for our times for, as W. E. Sangster reminds us, "We live in a world made grey by the atomic bomb." What can possibly better advertise the faith than a life lived with joy and the assurance that, even if the worst comes, one need not fear. The world is hungry for that kind of assurance and joy.

Fredrich Nietzsche, the German philosopher, whose ancestors on both sides were Lutheran ministers, at one time felt the appeal of the Christian faith and set himself to study it in the lives of some Christians he knew. But he was disappointed in their joyless natures and concluded, "These Christians will have to look more redeemed before I can believe in them!"

Something, then, in the Christian message can be *caught* as well as *taught*.

And now we come to the end of the day. Dedication had meant a call to purification, to a procession, to a proclamation, and finally to *provision*. This is implied in verse 44,

And at that time were some appointed over the chambers for

the treasures, for the offerings, for the firstfruits, and for the
tithes, to gather into them out of the fields of the cities the por-
tions of the law for the priests and Levites: for Judah rejoiced
for the priests and for the Levites that waited.

The glad spirit of that great day of dedication overflowed
and manifested itself in many ways. Here it provided suste-
nance for the Levites in their service. It is a true word, "The joy
of the Lord has many happy effects on the world, it also crowds
churches, fills treasuries, sustains various ministries, inspires
hymns of praise, and brings life and vigour into all the work of
religion."[7]

This is a basic biblical principle. It is better to give than to
receive. "There is that scattereth, and yet increaseth; and there
is that withholdeth more than is meet, but it tendeth to poverty"
(Prov 11:24). So wrote Solomon. The sad thing is that more
of us in the church of God do not see this. And if we do, we are
unwilling to act upon it.

Permit a personal word gleaned across three decades of
pastoral ministry. I have seen God work in this matter of giving. When I took up the work of my first church in Texas, I
held in sacred trust a word from J. Hudson Taylor, pioneer of
missions in China: "Depend upon it, God's work, done in God's
way, will never lack for God's supply." The Lord provided occasion for me to put that word to a rather severe test very early
in my ministry. My flock was small, less than one hundred.
The simple, new frame building that had been erected by my
predecessor had a long-term mortgage on it. The board was
careful how we distributed our limited funds lest we default on
the monthly payments. I appreciated their concern.

Then came the Second World War. Our young men being
sent overseas into a life and death struggle needed a source of
spiritual strength. The Gideons, a national organization committed to providing Bibles for hotels, determined to issue copies
of the New Testament to those in the armed forces who would

take them. Funds were gathered from member Gideons, and churches were urged to help. Our Texas Gideons urged me to consider the part that our small church might have in the program.

Subsequently I heard a speaker tell of servicemen who had been blessed by the Testaments. Some of them had received Christ. I was so impressed with this ministry that I asked him to bring a similar message to my congregation on his next visit to the city. For the occasion, a special display case holding 140 Testaments was built in the form of a cross. After the message, I appealed to my little flock for funds sufficient to purchase all 140. I did so with some anxiety, for the congregation was smaller than usual. But when the gifts were counted on my open Bible, we not only had enough to purchase the Testaments on display, we had enough to pay for 568. God had provided $142.13 that morning. So thrilled were all of us that we committed ourselves to provide at least five hundred Testaments every month as long as there was a need.

The sequel to that experience is even more remarkable. The zeal of my people did not slacken for many months following. Nor did their gifts. Offerings grew in excess of one thousand dollars month after month. Following our example, churches and men's Bible classes across the country took up the challenge, so that hundreds of thousands of New Testaments were distributed to our men overseas.

Meanwhile, what of our own work? The mortgage was paid off in less than three years; new property in downtown Houston was purchased; and the work prospered.

What God did in those early days has continued until now. I have learned that Jesus Christ is no thief. He will be no man's debtor. The appeal of Scripture is: "To do good and to communicate forget not: for with such sacrifices God is well pleased" (Heb 13:16).

12

Finally, Brethren, Farewell

Those familiar with the writings of the apostle Paul may recognize the title for this closing memoir; it is taken from the apostle's farewell to the Corinthian church (2 Cor 13:11).

For me the title has a contemporary association. For many years in my early ministry, I had a close friendship with Dr. William L. Pettingill, pastor, teacher, author, and one who, until his death in his eighties, was the last surviving coeditor of the *Scofield Reference Bible*.

Inevitably the time came for that grand old man to lay down the mantle of the pastorate. Deliberate as usual he prepared to close out his ministry at the First Baptist Church of New York and arranged that a certain Sunday would be his last. Accordingly he gave the church secretary his subjects for the coming Lord's day. The closing one was the farewell of Paul, referred to in the opening word of this study. But Dr. Pettingill never lived to preach that sermon. Reminiscent of Enoch of old, "God took him," as he prepared to make a telephone call in a hotel lobby.

So it came to pass that I had to take leave of a choice servant of Jesus Christ and a very dear personal friend.

We must now take leave of another choice servant and friend. At least I trust that by this time Nehemiah has become one of your biblical friends. This was one reason for this series of studies, for I have long felt that Nehemiah deserves to be better known and appreciated for his noble work.

110

As we come to this final memoir, I wish I could tell you without qualification that Nehemiah and his friends lived happily ever after. We would like to believe that, especially after viewing that great scene at the dedication of the wall. But we cannot do it, for the simple reason that "there is no finality in history." As Adeney has written so perceptively,

> The chapter that seems to be rounded off with a perfect conclusion always leaves room for an appendix, which in its time may serve as an introduction to another chapter. Ezra's and Nehemiah's work seemed to have reached its climax in the happy scene of the dedication of the walls. All difficulties had vanished; the new order had been greeted with widespread enthusiasm; the future promised to be smooth and prosperous. If the chronicler had laid down his pen at this point . . . his work might have presented a much more artistic appearance than it now wears. And yet it would have been artificial, and therefore false to the highest art of history. In adding a further extract from Nehemiah's memoirs that discloses a revival of the old troubles, and so shows that the evils against which the reformers contended had not been stamped out, the writer mars the literary effect of his record of their triumph; but, at the same time, he satisfies us that he is in contact with real life, its imperfections and its disappointments.[1]

This explains many things which happen in this life. It certainly explains many things which we find in our closing meditation.

Think of that good word just quoted from God's servant; what did he mean by the "old troubles" with which Nehemiah had to contend? And how did he and his colleagues purpose to deal with them? The answers to these questions are now provided by the memoir.

You will recall that in Nehemiah 9:38, the leaders and their people signed a "sure covenant" designed to deal with their domestic relationship to heathen nations in the matter of marriage, their commercial relationship in the matter of Sabbath

selling, and their spiritual relationship concerning the house of
God and those who served there. Looking now at the closing
excerpt from our friend's diary, we discover that that sure covenant was not sure!

What happened? Following the covenant signing and the
dedication service, Nehemiah left Jerusalem to return to Persia
and report to the king. As far back as Nehemiah 2:6, he had
told Artaxerxes of his desire to go to Jerusalem to rebuild the
wall. The king gave him permission, with the proviso that he
complete the project and return to the royal court. Nehemiah
understood this and "set him a time." Very likely, Nehemiah
was not able to give a specific date. We now know from his
own reference (5:14) that the total period of reconstruction
covered some twelve years. Having done his work, and having
served as nominal governor of Jerusalem, Nehemiah was now
constrained by conscience to return to Persia.

How long he remained away from Jerusalem is not clearly
indicated in the memoir. The text leaves the matter indefinite,
saying only, *"After certain days obtained I leave of the king:
And I came to Jerusalem"* (13:6-7).

When he returned, he discovered to his dismay that the old
troubles had spread like a cancer far and wide throughout
Judah. In verse 7, Nehemiah refers to one problem as "evil."
In the governor's absence the remnant had failed in much of
what had been promised. It appears that the leaders were particularly blameworthy for the defection of the people. Nehemiah found that Eliashib, the high priest, had provided Tobiah—that wretched scoundrel of earlier encounters, an asso-
ciate of Sanballat the Horonite—with an apartment in the
temple—furnished, mind you, by Tobiah!

Nehemiah records, *"And it grieved me sore: therefore I cast
forth all the household stuff of Tobiah out of the chamber"* (13:
8).

But this was not all that happened in the parish. Near the end
of the chapter, Nehemiah makes this further tragic entry, *"And*

one of the sons of Joiada, the son of Eliashib the high priest,
was son in law to Sanballat the Horonite: therefore I chased
him from me" (13:28).

Unfortunately, these incidents were only symptomatic of
more serious problems which had developed during Nehemiah's
absence. These problems were major matters about which the
people had taken firm action earlier. At verse 10, Nehemiah
records, *"And I perceived that the portions of the Levites had*
not been given them: for the Levites and the singers, that did
the work, were fled everyone to his field" (13:10).

Here was the initial evil: neglect of payments to the priests
and Levites. As a result, many of the sacred tribe were obliged
to go home and work their own fields for bare subsistence. The
remnant had defaulted in its pecuniary commitment to the
Lord. This failure was an index of the real condition of Israel's
heart. Their spiritual laxity and indifference were seen in their
effect on the treasury. It has been wisely commented that the
"financial thermometer is a very rough test of the spiritual condition of a religious community."[2]

Upon learning of this major dereliction of duty, Nehemiah
tells us, *"Then contended I with the rulers, and said, Why is the*
house of God forsaken? And I gathered them together, and set
them in their place" (13:11).

They apparently got a verbal lashing by the old reformer.
But he went beyond that. He established storehouses for the
corn, and the new wine, and oil. To assure the Levites and the
priests a continuous provision, he appointed Shelemiah, a priest,
Zadok, a scribe, and Pedaiah, a Levite, to distribute these provisions, and appointed with them one Hanun, a man of ap-
proved fidelity.

Why these men? Nehemiah tells us: *"for they were counted*
faithful" (13:13). It is interesting to see how often in the
sacred text faithfulness is set forward as the divine requirement
for service. It was so here.

The second indication of spiritual slippage is recorded at

verse 15. While touring the outlying districts of Judah, Nehemiah discovered that the people were violating their commitment by desecrating the Sabbath. This prompted a memorandum as follows,

> *In those days saw I in Judah some treading wine presses on*
> *the sabbath, and bringing in sheaves, and lading asses; as also*
> *wine, grapes and figs, and all manner of burdens, which they*
> *brought into Jerusalem on the sabbath day. . . . There dwelt*
> *men of Tyre also therein, which brought fish, and all manner*
> *of ware, and sold on the sabbath unto the children of Judah,*
> *and in Jerusalem* (13:15-16).

Once more, the reformer treated his own people and aliens
alike. He stopped the trade, closed the gates of the city, and
charged the Levites to keep them shut. One can almost hear
him issuing the order. The men of Tyre were not easily frightened however; they lodged outside the wall, and offered their
wares to the people. "Do that once more," said Nehemiah, "I
will lay hands on you!" (13:21, author's paraphrase). They
left after that. Thus by persuasion and vigorous action, the
governor put an end to that evil.

The final evidence of backsliding, and the one which may
have vexed Nehemiah's spirit more than the others, was the
problem of mixed marriages entered into despite the signed
covenant to preserve their God-given domestic relationship.
Here were Jews who, by taking wives of Ashdod, Ammon, and
Moab, had brought about relationships specifically forbidden
by the Lord in Deuteronomy 23:3. According to that divine
decree, no Ammonite or Moabite was to enter the congregation of Israel forever. Yet here they were, joined by the vow
of sacred marriage. The social and public mischief resulting
from these mixed marriages surfaced most distressingly in the
language of the Hebrew children. Nehemiah notes (13:24):
"And their children spake half in the speech of Ashdod, and

could not speak in the Jews' language, but according to the language of each people."

It was a mongrel tongue.

When Nehemiah heard those hated sounds, he simply lost his temper. With an oath, he rushed at the fathers, contended with them, smote some of them, plucked off their hair, and made them promise they would desist. In the end, he reminded them of Solomon: *"Was not this the sin of Solomon king of Israel? There was no king like him in all the nations; he was beloved by his God, and God made him king over all Israel. Yet even he was led into sin by his foreign wives"* (Neh 13:6, Moffatt).

The reformer prevailed, and there is reason to believe that idolatry received a death blow under Nehemiah's stern hand.

What is the abiding lesson of all these things? Certainly the Holy Spirit means that we learn well the importance of biblical separation from those things which are specifically forbidden by the Lord. It has been observed that indefiniteness forms no part of God's methods. His Word is definite. His commands are definite. His promises are definite. Therefore our obedience must be both intelligent and definite.

This is not an easy word for our time, for this is a day of compromise and indefiniteness with respect to almost every truth of Scripture. From the example of Nehemiah, I believe the message is clear: let those who sound the trumpets of God, whether the gospel to the world or the truth that edifies the people of God, see to it that they understand whereof they speak, and that they utter in no obscure or uncertain way the testimony of the Lord.

Nehemiah closes his noble diary with what seems to be his favorite telegraphic prayer, *"Remember me, O my God, for good"* (13:31). In fact he repeats, "Remember me, O my God," three times in this closing memoir (13:14, 22, 31).

What lay behind it all? Do we trace in that thrice-repeated

petition an undertone of melancholy? Was he simply giving
vent to his deep disappointment with the beloved people for
whom he had given so much and from whom he had received
so little? If this were his burden in prayer, we must not be hard
on him.

Nehemiah had suffered many things at the hands of enemies
and even brethren. Perhaps he was baring his heart and ac-
knowledging that it is indeed vain to trust in man. In his loneli-
ness and seeming failure, made to feel his insignificance and
limitations, Nehemiah turned to God, the one sure friend who
never forgets His own. He was not asking to purchase God's
favor; he wanted just the assurance of His *face* to satisfy him
that he had not labored in vain.

We know now that Nehemiah did not labor in vain. Faithful
courtier, true patriot, child of the court—yet patient in suffer-
ing hardships, inventive builder, impromptu general, astute
politician, high-spirited gentleman, inspired orator, resolute reformer, born leader among men: all these Nehemiah was.

It has been well said,

> Nehemiah, then, is not what hasty judges have called him,
> "one of the lesser lights." He is a gigantic figure that stalked
> across the page of history luminous, then glided into the dark
> abyss of time, but scattered sparks of historic light, and left,
> not one, but two immortal works behind him.[3]

We know those works well: his *wall* and his *writing.*

How glad we should be that this godly man said his say. Nehemiah's memoirs are immortalized as the book of Nehemiah
in the sacred library. As a result, he has ministered not only to
his own generation, but to generations following. Nehemiah
asked that God remember him for good. His prayer was won-
derfully answered.

Notes

INTRODUCTION

1. Bernhard W. Anderson, *Understanding the Old Testament,* p. 448.
2. Alexander Whyte, *Bible Characters: Ahithophel to Nehemiah,* p. 231.

CHAPTER 1

1. John F. Walvoord, *Israel in Prophecy,* pp. 19-20.
2. Viggo Olsen, *Daktar/Diplomat in Bangladesh,* pp. 323-24.
3. John C. Whitcomb, Jr., "Nehemiah," in *The Wycliffe Bible Commentary,* p. 435.

CHAPTER 2

1. Richard Ellsworth Day, *Filled with the Spirit,* p. 290.
2. Walter F. Adeney, "The Books of Ezra, Nehemiah, and Esther," in *The Expositor's Bible,* ed. W. Robertson Nicoll, 2:629.
3. Alexander Whyte, *Bible Characters: Ahithophel to Nehemiah,* p. 232.
4. Adeney, p. 629.
5. Ibid.
6. Ibid.
7. Ibid., p. 630.
8. Ibid., p. 631.
9. Ibid.
10. Ibid.
11. Ibid., p. 633.
12. Alexander Maclaren, "The Psalms," in *The Expositor's Bible,* ed. W. Robertson Nicoll, 3:138.
13. Adeney, p. 634.

CHAPTER 3

1. Walter F. Adeney, "The Books of Ezra, Nehemiah, and Esther," in *The Expositor's Bible,* ed. W. Robertson Nicoll, 2:635.
2. Ibid., p. 636.
3. Ibid., p. 638.
4. Ibid., p. 639.
5. Ibid., p. 640.

CHAPTER 4

1. Frank W. Boreham, *Bunch of Everlastings*, p. 138.
2. Walter F. Adeney, "The Books of Ezra, Nehemiah, and Esther," in *The Expositor's Bible*, ed. W. Robertson Nicoll, 2:644.
3. Ibid.
4. Ibid.
5. Ibid.
6. Ibid., p. 645.
7. Ibid.
8. Ibid.
9. Ibid., pp. 642-43.
10. Winston Churchill, "Give Me the Tools," *The Voice of Winston Churchill* (recording).

CHAPTER 5

1. Walter F. Adeney, "The Books of Ezra, Nehemiah, and Esther," in *The Expositor's Bible*, ed. W. Robertson Nicoll, 2:648.
2. Alexander F. Kirkpatrick, *The Book of Psalms*, p. 89.
3. J. Sidlow Baxter, *Mark These Men*, pp. 184-85.
4. Winston Churchill, "Their Finest Hour," *The Voice of Winston Churchill* (recording).

CHAPTER 6

1. *Unger's Bible Dictionary*, s.v. "Saint."
2. Edward Dennett, *Nehemiah . . . An Exposition*, pp. 51-52.
3. Roy L. Laurin, *I Corinthians: Where Life Matures*, p. 113.

CHAPTER 7

1. Charles Reade, *Bible Characters*, p. 43.
2. J. M. Randall, *Nehemiah the Tirshatha*, p. 110.
3. Reade, p. 46.
4. Walter F. Adeney, "The Books of Ezra, Nehemiah, and Esther," in *The Expositor's Bible*, ed. W. Robertson Nicoll, 2:654.
5. J. Sidlow Baxter, *Mark These Men*, p. 187.

CHAPTER 8

1. Robert Jamieson, A. R. Fausset, and David Brown, *A Commentary on the Whole Bible*, p. 297.
2. Edwin C. Deibler, Prologue to *Hymns of Jubilee*, comp. Richard H. Seume.
3. "Preface," in *Worship and Service Hymnal*, p. 2.

CHAPTER 9

1. Vance Havner, *Road to Revival*, p. 19.
2. Ibid., p. 23.
3. Walter F. Adeney, "The Books of Ezra, Nehemiah, and Esther," in *The Expositor's Bible*, ed. W. Robertson Nicoll, 2:655.
4. A. W. Tozer, *The Knowledge of the Holy*, p. 6.
5. Harry Allan Ironside, *Notes on Ezra, Nehemiah, and Esther*, p. 87.

CHAPTER 10

1. Alan Redpath, *Victorious Christian Service (Studies in the Book of Nehemiah)*, p. 156.
2. Walter F. Adeney, "The Books of Ezra, Nehemiah, and Esther," in *The Expositor's Bible*, ed. W. Robertson Nicoll, 2:662.
3. Ibid. p. 662.

CHAPTER 11

1. Walter F. Adeney, "The Books of Ezra, Nehemiah, and Esther," in *The Expositor's Bible*, ed. W. Robertson Nicoll, 2:669.
2. Ibid.
3. Ibid., pp. 669-70.
4. Ibid., p. 670.
5. Ibid.
6. Ibid., pp. 670-671.
7. Ibid., p. 671.

CHAPTER 12

1. Walter F. Adeney, "The Books of Ezra, Nehemiah, and Esther," in *The Expositor's Bible*, ed. W. Robertson Nicoll, 2:671.
2. Ibid., p. 672.
3. Charles Reade, *Bible Characters*, pp. 56-57.

Bibliography

Anderson, Bernhard W. *Understanding the Old Testament.* Englewood Cliffs, N.J.: Prentice-Hall, 1957.

Baxter, J. Sidlow. *Mark These Men.* Philadelphia: Westbrook, n.d.

Boreham, Frank W. *The Golden Milestone.* London: Epworth, 1961.

Day, Richard Ellsworth. *The Borrowed Glow.* Grand Rapids: Zondervan, 1938.

Deibler, Edwin C. Prologue to *Hymns of Jubilee,* edited by Richard H. Seume. Dallas: Dallas Theological Seminary, 1974.

Dennett, Edward. *Nehemiah (An Exposition).* London: G. Morrish, 1912.

Havner, Vance. *Road to Revival.* Philadelphia: Blakiston, 1940.

Ironside, Harry Allan. *Notes on Ezra, Nehemiah and Esther.* New York: Loizeaux, n.d.

Jamieson, Robert; Fausset, A. R.; and Brown, David. *A Commentary on the Whole Bible,* 2nd ed. Grand Rapids: Zondervan, n.d.

Kirkpatrick, A. F. *The Book of Psalms.* Cambridge: U. Press, 1894.

Laurin, Roy L. *I Corinthians: Where Life Matures.* 3rd ed. Findlay, Ohio: Dunham, 1957.

Nicoll, W. Robertson, ed. *The Expositor's Bible.* Vols. 2, 3. 2d ed. Grand Rapids: Eerdmans, 1940.

Olsen, Viggo. *Daktar/Diplomat in Bangladesh.* Chicago: Moody, 1973.

Reade, Charles. *Bible Characters.* New York: Harper, 1889.

Tozer, A. W. *The Knowledge of the Holy.* New York: Harper & Row, 1975.

Walvoord, John F. *Israel in Prophecy.* Grand Rapids: Zondervan, 1962.

Whyte, Alexander. *Bible Characters: Ahithophel to Nehemiah.* Edinburgh and London: Oliphants, 1903.

RECORDINGS

Churchill, Winston. "Give Me the Tools." On *The Voice of Winston Churchill.* England: Decca Record Company, side 1.
———. "Their Finest Hour." On *The Voice of Winston Churchill.* England: Decca Record Company, side 1.